Rev. H H Goodell
Steger, Ill.

THE

DIMENSION

✳✳✳

OF DEPTH

❈❈❈❈❈❈❈❈❈❈❈❈❈❈❈❈❈❈❈❈❈❈❈❈❈❈❈❈❈❈❈❈

Other Books by the Same Author

Coming to Terms with the Universe
Jesus and the Liberal Mind
Rev. John Doe, D.D.
Thunder Over Sinai
The Social Manifesto of Jesus
These Shared His Passion
These Shared His Cross
These Shared His Power
Four Freedoms and God
Last Reprieve?
God Makes the Difference
Mandate to Humanity

Poetry

Centurion (a dramatic narrative poem)
Over the Sea, the Sky

THE

DIMENSION

OF

DEPTH

BY Edwin McNeill Poteat

HARPER & BROTHERS

PUBLISHERS

NEW YORK

DEDICATED TO

Carlyle, Susan,

and McNeill III

CONTENTS

ACKNOWLEDGMENTS

The author gratefully acknowledges the courtesy of the following publishers for the use of copyrighted references used in this book: Rinehart & Co., Harper & Brothers, The Saturday Review, The Atlantic Monthly, Charles Scribner's Sons, The Macmillan Company, The World Publishing Co., Bobbs-Merrill. All the scripture quotations are from the Revised Standard Version, Thomas Nelson & Sons, publishers.

Also to the good-humored and diligent assistance of Mrs. Betsy Senter Wooden in the preparation of the manuscript.

E.M.P.

That the last six weeks of our Lord's earthly life are more amply remembered and recorded than any other segment of his experience is clear, even to the casual reader. This detail is accounted for first by the fact that they were days that showed a decline in popular favor. Considerable distance had been covered since the first spectacular events that accompanied the beginning of his ministry. Except for the final journey to Jerusalem, in which much of the crowd acclaim was little more than the focus of a general holiday excitement on an interesting and momentarily exciting person, those who followed him became fewer and fewer. At one distressful point it is recalled that he turned and asked the members of the inner circle if they too were not "going away." The ready response of Peter seems to have been immensely, though only for a moment, reassuring.

This factor of diminishing popular following is not only explicit in the record, it appears to have accounted for the emphasis given to his teaching. He could not confront the collapse of his movement—as the Jordan Valley movement of John the Baptist had collapsed—without thinking and speaking in terms of crisis.[1] But crisis invites more than the selection of theme; it supplies intensity. This concentration,

[1] A detailed discussion of this forms the body of the author's *Parables of Crisis,* Harper, 1950.

as in the parables with which the period abounds, is expressed in his occupation with ideas focused so sharply as to make them inescapable and yet so portentous as to compel sustained reflection. To use a somewhat unsavory simile: the more precise the pin-pointing, the more important the target.

"Great indeed, we confess, is the mystery of our religion" (I Tim. 3:16, r.s.v.) or, as Moffat renders it: "And who does not admit how profound is the divine truth of our religion?" The mystery of our religion is confessed, in our times, by few; its mystification is generally acknowledged. This, paradoxically, in spite of the endless simplifications to which it has been reduced in plans of salvation, creeds, confessions and proof texts. If we honestly answer the proposition as Moffat puts it in question form, we must say we can give the names of many who do not "admit how profound is the divine truth of our religion." They do not admit that it is profound at all. They think it is what our do-it-yourself forebears called "a simple," meaning an easily brewed herb medicine the properties of which were thought able to cure any ailment.

To read the story of the last days of Jesus' life is to discover that he was not brewing simples for indiscriminate dispensing. Moving, as he was, into those heavily shadowed areas of experience in which his commitment to the Father's purposes was to be tested to the uttermost, he explored the dimension of depth which alone reveals the profundity and the mystery of our religion. What he said was offered to those who needed to have their religious faith deepened. Many defected; it was easier to think of a return of David to a throne too long unoccupied; it was simpler to bring a sacrifice to the Temple. A house built on sand *might* withstand the shock of storm; at any rate it could be quicker built and sooner occupied than one with a rock foundation. This depthless understanding is still characteristic of our simple religion, our shallow or sand-supported commitments.

In the following reflections the effort is made to plumb once again the dimension of depth out of which his words rose darkly to the surface, and are the result of the repetition of an annual pilgrimage the author has for many years made in imagination during the last journey south.[2] Generally speaking, the hearts of concerned Christians are more sensitive during Lent than at any other period of the Christian year. For this reason it is possible to introduce them to "the mystery of our religion"; to lead them into deeper waters, to take them literally out beyond their depth.

For this is what the Gospels show us Jesus doing. The Moffatt book skillfully winds together the narrative thread that runs through the Synoptics and the Fourth Gospel, aware of the difficulty that Biblical specialists find in the historicity of the letter. Thus in our studies we make a

[2] The guide on this tour has mostly been *Everyman's Life of Jesus: A Narrative in the Words of the Four Gospels,* edited by James Moffatt, Harper, 1925.

natural, though confessedly arbitrary, grouping of ideas: Jesus sees himself, the demands of discipleship and the understanding of the ultimate issues of life all within the dimension of their true depth.

We are not allowed to think that it was not until the last journey south that he began, for himself, this deeper searching. It is rather that the exigent pressures of the situation—political, social, religious and personal—into which he had moved made it imperative that he sharpen the focus, plumb the deep, reveal the mystery, for those who still walked by his side. They were bewildered, distrustful and disappointed. Our Lord had two alternatives: he could either soothe them with palliatives, which might have appeared more kind even though it would have evinced a superficial diagnosis; or he could take them with him into the depths, knowing that only those who have ventured the profundity of the deeps can feel the ecstasy of the heights. This latter he did. And as they walked with him through the mortal night they emerged with him into the deathless dawn.

THE

DIMENSION

✳✳

OF DEPTH

JESUS SEES HIMSELF

IN THE DIMENSION

OF DEPTH

Part I

1 THE LOGIC OF BELIEF

You believe in God; believe also in me. JOHN 14:1

It is not necessary to our purpose to discuss fully the self-consciousness of Jesus. This has invited speculation ever since the majesty of his personality was first evident. It has been little more than speculation for the reason that no one can know the self-consciousness of another. No matter how we may try, the result is almost entirely a projection of oneself on to another plus, perhaps, a measure of wishful thinking. If this transference is true of our experience with our fellows, it must have been so with his friends. "What sort of man is this, that even winds and sea obey him?" (Matt. 8:27).

That he was not really known to them, or at best known only on superficial levels, seems indicated by the necessity he felt a few hours before his death for a final identification of himself. "Have I been with you so long, and yet you do not know me, Philip?" (John 14:9). There might have been an inflection of exasperation in that question. To be sure, there are ways in which much of what we are is always concealed even from those who have been with us the longest. It is important that we remind ourselves of this barrier to complete understanding so that when we are misunderstood we can forbear to criticize. Remember the mote and the beam.

Whether Jesus was impatient with Philip, and the others for whom he most certainly was the spokesman, we need not inquire. What is clear from the record is that he responded sympathetically to their bewilderment and tried to identify himself in a deeper dimension of being and understanding.

(1)

There are two methods, the logicians tell us, by which a proposition may be logically established. One starts from a particular fact and moves toward a general conclusion about all relevant facts. Thus: the smallest thing that Democritus could think of was an indivisible particle, that thing within which further differentiation was impossible. To this he gave the name ATOM, *a:* not, $+$ *tomos:* to cut. He projected this hunch as far as his mind could reach and concluded that the universe was made up of these particles, each indivisible but capable of combining with others in infinite variety. Nowadays we know that the atom *is* divisible; that it is a constellation of positive, negative and neutral radioactive entities. We project that idea to infinity and conclude that the universe is composed of electromagnetic energy in an infinite and orderly dance.

This method of inquiry is described as induction; it begins with the small and moves to the large; it begins with the particular and argues toward the general.

A second method is described as deductive. This begins with a generalization and moves toward the particular. Discover the pattern, deduce the details. The vast is set before us in order that we may apprehend the minute. Thus we may set forth the proposition that the large-scale cosmic operation is orderly; there is nothing capricious or slipshod in the cyclic processional of the stars. Therefore, we go on to infer, man, as a part of the cosmos, is a part of a cosmic order. At least within the physical aspects of my life I am subject to laws the keeping of which makes me an orderly person.

(2)

To read our text as an indication that Jesus was applying the method of deductive reasoning in an effort to identify himself is to put something into his words that is not there. Nevertheless, it is not without interest to note that when a situation arose in which the incredulity of his friends made necessary the choice of a method of dealing with their problem, he started with God in order to make himself credible. On another occasion he invited the still unpersuaded Thomas to touch him, to feel his flesh that his realness might be manifest. In the instance we are considering, however, he got as far from himself as a man can get: he went to the uttermost limit to God, to prove his immediate self. Believe in God; believe also (or therefore) in me. This seems to fit the pattern of deductive reasoning.

This process excludes no other method of reasoning that in other ways is helpful. Tennyson was sure that from a flower he could convince himself—if he knew enough about it—as to "what God and man is."

We incline to think, however, that for the greater part, men incline to assume the general fact of God as the major premise for understanding and identifying themselves. God may be given no end of names: Prime Mover—thus Aristotle; Dialectic Materialism—thus Marx; Heaven—thus Confucius; the Way— thus Lao Tze; Father—thus the Hebrew-Christian tradition. That each of these carries its own shade of meaning and emphasis does not disqualify the fact that each is an effort to give a name to a general concept: a concept in relation to which one seeks to identify oneself.

In the case of our Lord, the name God had its special—we might even say, its private—meaning. God was the Creator, Sustainer, Judge and Redeemer of the World. He was a Father of exhaustless patience and compassion. Better still, He was always at hand to those who, impoverished by sin, were hungry and thirsty for righteousness. To compose these attributes into a general concept of God was the great spiritual achievement of the seers of Israel. God was to them the mighty fact; it was from this titan generalization that man's partialities were deduced and understood.

(3)

And Jesus went on to say that because of this great central affirmation, it was proper to deduce something about himself. "Believe in God; believe also in me." Would he have said: If you don't believe in God you cannot believe in me? Perhaps; but more of that in a moment.

Now the reason that this is called an identification in depth is that it expands at once the dimensions within which he set himself. He was not, we think, making a deduction about his actual physical existence. That was unnecessary: there he stood in the company of his friends and there was no need for a demonstration of his physical actuality. That necessity was felt decades later when some believers maintained that his physical realness was a fantasy.

If this is so, then he must have been asking them to make deductions about something other than his physique. Such an inference had to do, not with his existence but with his qualities—the nature and essence of his spirit. So, if this surmise is to be put in familiar terms, we seem to hear him saying that

from the nature and spirit of God it was possible—and logical—
to deduce the nature and spirit of himself.

In a manner of speaking, it is axiomatic that God cannot be
different from His creatures. This is the obverse face of the
equally axiomatic proposition that He is wholly other than His
creatures. The deep mystery of creation lies in this merciless
paradox. Our puzzled inquiries as to the origin of evil will find
no satisfaction here, or, indeed, the question of good.

Nevertheless, there is at least the partial truth that divine
creative activity could not involve the contradiction implicit in
God's creating something wholly different—to the point of con-
trariety—from Himself. Thus we say that God is somehow in
everything we see and know. However troublesome this idea
may become we cannot give way to its opposite; namely, that
all we see and know is alien to, or at enmity with, the Creator.

As this relation of God to His creation involves what we have
been hearing Jesus say, it would seem then that because God is
creative, merciful, just, redemptive, Jesus, who was His son
was also creative, merciful, just, redemptive. Logically speaking, because of the nature of the general, we deduce the nature
of the particular. You believe in what God is, believe therefore
in what I am.

To be sure, Jesus did not spell it out in these terms but it is
likely that those to whom he was speaking would have understood. How, indeed, is God, whose being is unknowable, to be
known otherwise than through His essences? And this, manifestly, is what is generally meant when it is said that Jesus is
like God; or, arguing inductively as is as often done, that God
is like Jesus.

Furthermore, this is what is meant by the logic of belief or
the logical relation between Jesus and God. It is central to the
Christian witness and should support resistance to the critical
assaults and peripheral uncertainties that are so often disturbing

to many of his devoted followers; such matters, for example, as the physical generation of Jesus and the relation of that process to God.

(4)

It is important to point out a logical extension of this identification between Jesus and God. Is it not the only logical ground upon which man can have a reasonable belief in man? You believe in God; believe also in man. This is a great deal easier than arguing that because we believe in man we therefore must believe in God. God may be, as some have insisted, no more than the projection of a father-image. That would do also for our concept of the devil, if we had the wrong kind of father.

And yet it is suggestive to observe the correlation between atheism and misanthropy. Not always, to be sure; presumably there are those whose disbelief in God is compensated for by a profound belief in humanity. This optimist is part of the picture of naturalistic humanism. We cannot be dogmatic at this point, yet there is something to be said for the idea that those who have found no need for God can most easily dispense with their need of men. Gas chambers offer grisly confirmation of this misanthropy. Indeed, is not godlessness the reason and justification of selfishness, a devotion to self that ironically tends to elevate the self to the status of deity?

Having said that, and indeed in apparent contradiction, we suggest the final logical extension of this identification in depth. Believe in God; believe also in yourself! Dare we say this? Manifestly this is not the sin of self-deification just referred to; it is simply the only justification that man has for believing in himself. My belief in God provides the logic for my belief in myself. Of course if one has lost belief in himself, logic will perhaps offer him meager reassurance. Yet if we do humbly and honestly believe in ourselves—as we must believe in others—is this not primarily because we believe in God? Man's belief in himself because of himself is pride, a shallow, profitless thing; man's belief in himself because of his belief in God is—or may be—an identification in depth, the worth of which is beyond all computing.

When God was banished in the French Revolution, human life cheapened. What becomes of individual dignity where the State is the only deity to which man can bow down? If we do not believe in man, can we truly believe in God? If we believe in God, must we not truly believe in man? If we believe in God and man, may we not safely believe in ourselves?

"You believe in God; believe also in me." The mystery of the Christian movement is hidden, perhaps, in the fact that those who heard this identification in depth heeded it, and all of life for them and through them moved into a new dimension. Is it too much to assume then that in our dealings with ourselves, our fellows, our Christ, our God, a recovery of depth for each of these areas of action and thought would enrich our minds and enliven our hearts with new devotion?

2 THE LOGIC OF SIGHT

He who has seen me has seen the Father. JOHN 14:9

We have made use of the pattern of deductive logic in attempting to understand Jesus' identification of himself with God. In our second study we discover him identifying God with himself. The philosophers, we are told, reason deductively; the scientist reasons inductively and we are here confronted with an inductive identification in depth.

Deductive logic starts with the general and moves to the particular; inductive reason reverses the direction, beginning with the particular and moving toward the general. Or, in the language of our text; beginning with what is *seen* one argues the reality of what is *not seen*. This, for reasons of convenience, we have called the logic of sight.

It is easy to see why science uses the inductive method. Science does business with what is seen. With the eye, of course, but also with the other senses, since we see—meaning we take in—by means of the total sensorium. How elaborate the mechanisms for this seeing have become: the Palomar telescope that scans billions of space miles, the electronic microscope that enlarges the invisible twenty thousand times, the radar beam that "sees" the out-of-sight object and blips its location on a screen, the sonar high-frequency wave that ranges the deeps and "hears" the distant submarine or the nearby shark, the photoelectric plate that reproduces the shadow track cast by the flight of a split atom.

However clear these sensory apprehensions may be, there is still a mystery about seeing. How implicitly can we trust our sight? This is not a matter simply of optics; confidence is not to be established by the correction of faulty vision. What we look at provides us only a little—some would argue it provides nothing—of what we see. So preponderant is the seer in what is reported as having been seen that the witness to an act, or indeed to a thing, must be corroborated endlessly before approximate certitude can be had. A recently published anthology of one hundred and six pieces about New York City [1] exhibits uniformity only in the diversity of what each writer sees in the great metropolis.

This is no reason for distrust or for cynicism; it is rather the reason for the caution that the scientist brings to his seeing. For if he is guilty of a mistake in apprehending the fact, the generalization he makes will be wrong and may be dangerous.

(1)

This formula for seeing has bearing on what Jesus was saying about himself to his bewildered friends. Here he is not arguing from the reality—or the nature—of God to his own nature, and inferentially to the nature of humankind. He is arguing from the particular, the observable, fact of himself to the existential fact of the Father. "He who has seen me has seen the Father." Here we must give to the word "seen" the dimensions within which it can be most fruitfully understood.

He had been with them "so long" and they had seen him constantly and intimately. He was Jesus of Nazareth, their friend and leader, whose every feature and mannerism was familiar to them. This was important for them, and yet the

[1] Alexander Klein, ed., *The Empire City: A Treasury of New York,* Rinehart & Co., 1955.

most important fact about him they had not seen—that he was the Father.

We are not concerned at this point with the theological implications of this astonishing idea for the reason that we doubt that it was "seen" theologically. Their problem was God; they wanted proof, not merely evidence, that He existed. With all that their friend had told them about God, he had failed to make Him visible. It is apparent from the record that they thought he was able to do just that. "Show us the Father, and we shall be satisfied." If this was not a taunt it was plaint and, we must assume, from their point of view, wholly reasonable.

Indeed, is it not justified from almost any point of view? A sight of God is what everyone wants. Even those least worthy to look on Him—and who of us is worthy?—would secretly exult in an authentic vision of the Divine. It might not satisfy us; on the contrary it might do the opposite—dissatisfy us with the sight of everything else, including our own wretched selves.

This desire to "see" God may be no more than one of those correspondences that we note between ourselves and our environment. As the eye is correlative to light, the ear to vibration, the lung to air, so man's inner need for God seeks correspondence in what he thinks he can identify as God.

We may be quite sure that the wish to see God is the explanation of man's tireless industry in making images, in the worship of visible things, and in the symbolism of language, all of which are efforts to hypostatize God, to give Him substance, a reality we can "see." Our five senses report in such detail the physical world about us that we make a God that these seemingly indefatigable and ingenious senses can apprehend. This perception, to be sure, is subject to abuse and needs constant examination lest image be made identical with, instead of representative of, the thing that eludes our sensory grasp. Despite proscriptions against imaging God man will always imagine him in terms of familiar sense experience. God is an image-maker, says the Genesis story. So is man and perhaps for the same reason.

(2)

The logic of sight, or the inductive process, seems, at this point, to say that through the gate of the eye—or the total seeing mechanism—there come identifications which help our adjustment to the external world. The degree of accuracy in seeing varies, and depends on factors that can be more or less measured and corrected. But sightless eyes, no matter how blindness may be compensated for by the heightened acuity of our other organs of sense, are a barrier to full understanding. To paraphrase the words of Philip: if we could only have a certification of God by a glimpse of the Father, what a satisfaction that would be. To which Jesus replied in the words of our text: "He who has seen me has seen the Father."

(3)

To some this has the ring of intolerable self-assertiveness. It might be said that Jesus as an egotist would logically be the greatest of all braggarts. Others who are unaccustomed to the Christian testimony have said his claim is the quintessence of blasphemy. We have no way of knowing how far his answer to Philip was satisfying. The record lacks the very point toward which the story seemed to be moving. We shall see in another connection that Jesus adduced not only himself but his words and his works as identifying him with God. Indeed he seemed willing, in default of credibility on other grounds, to rest his claim on his works: "Or else believe me for the sake of the works themselves" (John 14:11).

We may take this ambiguity to intimate that Philip was *not* convinced of the reality of God simply by a sight of Jesus. Yet this uncertainty should not be laid as a charge against Philip. His difficulty was our own: he could not really *see* Jesus. There he stood as a man, a familiar friend; but seeing him thus did not open to sight the vision of God. Why? Because a sight of God is not apprehensible by the five senses, or even by a sixth, if there be one.

This is the heart of the mystery of Incarnation; it is also the reason why the logic of sight does not ultimately persuade. "Blessed are those who have not seen and yet believe." We remember the words quoted earlier: "Who does not admit how profound is the divine truth of our religion?" This should not discomfit us overmuch. What our Lord was trying to do was not to make a syllogism that would convince but to make an identification of himself in depth that would constrain.

(4)

It is just this larger dimension that is necessary to us for it suggests an attitude of mind that should have practical bearing on our distressful days. We speak theologically of THE incarnation and upon it erect a structure of great impressiveness. To understand Jesus in depth may make it possible to enlarge our concept of incarnation, though it may call for some new sort of accommodation within our prevailing theological framework. It may on the contrary be regarded as lying wholly out of bounds to theology.

Nevertheless, it is our feeling that nothing is taken from the mystery and grandeur of the words of our text when we say that in a very real way they apply also to ourselves. Our spiritual sensitiveness will feel a shock when we hear ourselves say: he that has seen me has seen the Father. Should not so impious a mouth be choked with dust? Perhaps. And yet this can be said without pretending to appear as walking demonstrations of divinity. Here the fine line that divides between candor and pride is easily overstepped and folly will rush in where humility fears to tread. But is it not true that in much the same way in which we see God who "plants his footsteps in the sea and rides upon the storm" we look at man and see God?

At this point we need to remember the limits within which all our seeing is set. We must resort to metaphor if we are to see God's footsteps in the sea. Whoever traced footprints in water? But metaphor is often a way of deepening our seeing. Is not incarnation itself a metaphor of measureless depth?

What was it in the religious culture of our Lord that was most clearly representative of God? The Eternal was *seen* in the natural world but He was not *proved* by it. It was in the spirit of man that He was manifest. God was not *in* the fire or the earthquake; He was *in* the small voice, a voice inaudible to any except Elijah. Nowhere in the Old Testament do we have the daring metaphor of incarnation, but the Eternal Word is set forth in countless other metaphors. It is the Word spoken by man rather than the Word enfleshed in the Son of Man; man is the vessel that contains rather than the body that incarnates. The metaphor of embodiment is more Greek than Hebrew.

One scarcely escapes the diffusiveness of the God-is-Everywhere idea except by the sense that God is truly in one's heart; just as one avoids the loneliness of the God-is-Out-There by "seeing" Him in the life of another. "Where pity dwells the peace of God is there," says Whittier. Not the peace that is the result of pity given and accepted, but the peace that is the essence of God. We cannot claim that every impulse to compassion, forgiveness, justice, mercy, inquiry, sacrifice, is the secretion of endocrine glands, the result of body chemistry. The discredited scientific humanism that a generation ago totted up man's value in terms of ninety-nine cents' worth of chemicals may have produced something akin to a sense of humility, but it was as distorted as our easy boasts that all our spiritual qualities are of our own contriving.

To say that he who has seen man has seen God is of course far from the whole story. Too often to look at a man is to see a hideous perversion of all that God means. This is due partly to human sin and partly to our faulty seeing. For we can no more "see" a man than Philip could look at Jesus and "see" God!

All this may have a practical value within the orbit of personal and group relations today. It is easy to divide men into friends and enemies and to give the latter all the compounded vices and evils we all loathe. Suppose, however, that we could honestly say—and believe the logic of sight—that he who has seen a Russian peasant has seen God or—and this would take colossal faith or opaque blindness—that he who has seen the leader of Red China has seen God.

This might foul up our theology; we are not yet ready for what might be called a universal incarnationism. But in the imaginative projection of the Last Judgment in the twenty-fifth of Matthew, we are confronted with incarnations of God that had been naked, and sick, and hungry, and imprisoned. And those who ministered to their misery had also been incarnations of the Father. This is metaphor, to be sure, but so also, as we have said, is incarnation itself.

Why did Jesus bid his friends turn the other unsmitten cheek to the enemy? To be dramatic? Or foolhardy? Or was it because he saw identification in depth, he could see something of God in the enemy himself, something awesome and abysmal but something which alone could provide the ground of reconciliation if the wish for it were in the heart?

3 THE LOGIC OF IDENTITY

Believe me that I am in the Father and the Father in me. JOHN 14:11

We must not lose sight of the fact that in the profound words of our Lord considered here we see an effort on his part to convey to his friends a deeper understanding of himself than they seem hitherto to have had. That there was a need for deeper understanding is distressing. They had been with him "so long" and yet had not known him. How then are we, who, though we may say we have known him longer, yet known him less intimately, to be sure of him?

To believe in him because we believe in God is not difficult; to "see" God because we have "seen" Jesus is, perhaps, less simple because our seeing, at best, is faulty. The proposal contained in our text, however, seems to increase rather than simplify the problem. At the same time we must think that he was trying to clarify their bewilderment by deepening their understanding.

The difficulty he had in enlarging the dimension within which he was to be known without losing them altogether in an abyss of confusion is seen by the word "identity" which we use. There is, we assume, a logic of identity. If A is identical with B we logically deduce a close relation between them. But close relation does not mean identity, necessarily; it may mean sameness and no more. Identical twins are not really identical, they are only very, very much alike. This explanation falls in line with what we have been saying about the use of metaphor. Metaphor suggests likeness between fact and idea. "The wings of the morning" is an imaginative picture of the way the morning may be thought to move toward us. It is *like* something with tinted, titan wings. But when we say that, we are far from identifying the slow turning of the earth toward the sun's fixed light with the beating of luminous pinions beneath the horizon's dawn-lit contours.

(1)

Now it is important to see that when Jesus says "I am in the Father and the Father in me" he is using the language of metaphor. We have called this the logic of identity simply because there is no more precise word to be had. But had he been using the language of fact he would have said: "I am the Father and the Father is I." That such an identification as that is cherished or demanded by many is not our point here. What we are trying to say is that any true identification of God as Jesus, and vice versa, is a matter of metaphysics; it has to do with the being and essence of both. The intrusion of the little preposition "in" is what makes the statement metaphorical. Pure being is independent of place and time; it has no in-ness, so when we speak of it as *in* something we are speaking in metaphor.

This distinction should be made clearer by observing that if it were possible for one person—or thing—to be in (meaning co-spatial) someone else, individual identity would be hidden or lost. In human experience this fact is fairly simple. Geometry tells us two objects cannot occupy the same space at the same time. In the relationship between Jesus and the Father, because of established theological ideas, it *is* possible. But the metaphorical as contrasted with the metaphysical is suggested when we give to "in" the somewhat more specific connotation "inside." Here is pure metaphor: to say that Jesus was inside the Father, and vice versa, is to understand the statement in terms of location and not of identity since "in" refers to space or time, twin categories within which pure being cannot be understood.

(2)

Jesus, we have insisted, was trying to help his friends understand him within deeper dimensions. This acceptance could not have been easy; very few of us are so insistent on getting to the bottom of things that a shallow explanation will not satisfy us. And we may properly assume that if Jesus ever was concerned with metaphysical explanations of himself, he must long since have discovered that his friends were not. The question—or demand—of Philip, "Show us the Father," and the promise, "We will be satisfied," is proof enough of that. "Show us" did not mean "present us with an argument."

Since he was trying to deal with them on a level where they could grasp his meaning, what are we to make of this metaphor of location? We must dismiss metaphysical suggestions as irrelevant at this point and try to see how metaphor illumines the proposition. This is done, we have been saying, by his deepening of the dimension within which he was to be seen.

Where was Jesus when he was confronted with the challenge of Philip? He was *in* Jerusalem and *in* the last week of his mortal life. These locations inside space and time were clear and identifiable. And they can be broken down into other more specific identifications. He was *in* a family to which he was affiliated; *in* a group to which he was allied; *in* an upper room, a society, a nation, a culture, a race, a species, a cosmos. He was *in* the time of the Passover festival, *in* the evening, *in* the thirtieth year of his life, *in* the reign of Tiberius Caesar, *in* the first century, *in* history.

There are also still deeper levels of in-ness: he was *in* trouble, meaning that the retreat of the multitudes, the signs of defection within the disciple group, his suspicion of treachery and the certainty of his own death which he tried to share with his friends, these placed him *in* a situation—we might even say *in* a state of mind that, while profound, was clearly discernible even by the most obtuse of his associates.

When, however, he said "I am *in* the Father and the Father *in* me" he was moving into depths that to this hour are yet unplumbed. Thus it is only by metaphor that we can approach an understanding of the words.

As if he was aware of this difficulty he appears to have prepared his friends somewhat by speaking of words and authority and works: "The words that I say to you I do not speak on my own authority; but the Father who dwells in me does his works" (John 14:10). Here were matters they could grasp; his words they had heard and to them they were the words of eternal life; they had seen his works: "What mighty works are wrought by his hands!" (Mark 6:2). And even those least friendly to him were impressed with his authority, not the scribelike sort but something so virile as to cause wonder, admiration and not a little misgiving.

All of this: word, authority, work, he said, was God *in* him. To those whose religious culture was based on the audibility of the word of God, the visibility of the work of God and the inescapability of the authority of God, these familiar words made sense. It was what all the prophets had claimed; it was what gave to the prophetic witness both its passion and its tenderness. A later spokesman for God was to say: "God is at work in you, both to will and to work for his good pleasure" (Phil. 2:13).

(3)

It is no doubt as difficult for us to realize that God is at work in us as it was for Jesus' friends to understand that he was in the Father and the Father in him. And this is due to the metaphysical problem—shall we say?—of one person being in another person. That this is no problem to the mystic does not help us who lack the mystic's sensitivity. Nevertheless, there is a way in which it is easy to understand this as fact as well as metaphor.

Consider the way, for example, one's physical parents are *in* him. Here is mystery enough, to be sure; and genetics has still to solve all the problems of heredity, that microscopic bridge across which parent moves to child, child to parent, and generation to generation. By what magic is the unique note of the wood thrush, sung always at dawn and twilight, transmitted by chromosomes from bird to egg to bird? Those who know the thrush identify the invariable sound, and can almost anticipate the invariable moment.

It is the same magic that passes along the color of eye and hair from parent to child; aptitudes for living, perhaps, nerve cells weak or strong for responding to the grimness or the grandeur of life. You are the spit and image of your father, or your mother—so we put it and state a biological fact and more, if we see life deeply enough. It is the logic of identity through an identification that dissolves nothing of the individuality which, as we have already noted, is immutably discontinuous with identity.

So much for the testimony of heredity; we do have our parents in us; "The Father is in me." Is it possible in somewhat the same way to say that we are also in our parents? Is not the discontinuity between child and parent, despite inherited traits, so final that it cannot be said that the child is in the parent? What did Wordsworth mean by saying "the child is father of the man"?

Not biologically, of course; but spiritually. Ask any mother: when she says her child is forever in her heart she is not mawkish. Ask any father: when he says his child is forever in his hopes he is not sentimental. And the point of this normal human response is that it conceives of the parent-child relationship in depth. Here is something as mysterious in its way as chromosomes and far more profound. For only as this sort of identity (remembering the word's limitations) is sustained can the child-parent relation escape shallowness, cheapness, and evanescence.

We have mentioned the mystical experience, that sense of absorption into the Divine which seems beyond the reach of most of us. It is described by Louis de Blois, who was born a Flemish aristocrat in the sixteenth century but by choice became a Benedictine monk: "It is to start right now to be a partaker *in* Divinity, to be a child of God. Right now, and through all eternity, continually rising upward, more and more moving, more and more thunderous, not toward God, but *in* God, *in* the very essence of the limitless." [1] It is said that W. E. Gladstone and other prominent lay figures in England were greatly influenced by this saintly man. Would it have appeared presumptuous for them to think of themselves as being *in* God? Louis speaks of "continually rising upward"; we have been speaking of identification in depth. Whether up or down, no matter. Each, we point out again, is the language of metaphor. And it is used, we think, because there is some inner urgency in the religious aspiration that compels us toward more and more spacious dimensions of the spirit leading us into "the very essence of the limitless."

[1] Quoted by Margaret Applegarth in *Moment by Moment*, Harper, 1955.

We have earlier said that to believe in God should help us to believe in man and in ourselves; and that to say "he that has seen me has seen the Father" provides us a dimension within which our self-awareness may become both the apprehension and forth-showing of God. To exalt either of these is the sin of pride; to repudiate either is the sin of self-abandonment. For this reason we feel that Jesus, as he undertook to identify himself in depth, was not only showing something of himself to his friends but showing his friends something about themselves they needed to know; something perhaps that would save them from both pride and low aim.

As a matter of fact this is precisely what seems to have happened. "God is at work *in* you," Paul wrote his friends at Philippi. There is no difficulty here for us; numerous experiences prompt us to feel that in ways beyond (deeper than) our understanding and design, God is at work in persons, in situations, in processes. If the reverse—I in God—is more difficult it may be because modern sophistication does not encourage the plunge, yet it was not forbidding to earlier times. Paul, speaking in the Areopagus, first reminded his Athenian listeners: "Yet he [God] is not far from each one of us"; and then went beyond the proximity of God to God as the dimension within which "we live and move and have our being" (Acts 17:27-28).

The most startling metaphor of all identifies in depth the disciple and his Lord. "He who eats my flesh and drinks my blood abides in me, and I in him" (John 6:56). How mischievous the consequences of that have been when the figure of speech has been understood as a statement of fact! Observe also the favorite analogy of the First Letter of John: "By this we may be sure that we are in him: he who says he abides in him ought to walk in the same way he walked" (I John 2:5-6). And: "All who keep his commandments abide in him, and he in them" (I John 3:24).

This interpretation must all be set within the last few days when Jesus and his friends felt the tensions tightening between him and them, and between them and the crowds. It was needful for him to help them understand him. This he did by setting himself within the dimensions "of the limitless." It was the logic of identity to which he appealed as his ultimate credential.

The report of the conversation between Philip and Jesus does not indicate how successful the effort was. What we find, however, is that within the Christian fellowship, after the resurrection experience, the logic of identification was both understood and appropriated. Those who had found him to be in the Father and the Father in him took the daring step Louis de Blois described: ". . . continually rising upward, more and more moving, more and more thunderous, not toward God, but *in* God, in the very essence of the limitless." That may help us explain the dynamism of the first Christian fellowship.

How confidently can we say, "Believe me that I am in the Father and the Father in me"? And what does that show us about the Christian fellowship today?

4 THE LOGIC OF WORK

Or else believe me for the sake of the works themselves. JOHN 14:11

In connection with this fourth approach that Jesus made in the effort to help his friends understand him, an earlier reference to the logic of works should be helpful. To deduce Jesus from the hypothesis of God; to see God by seeing him; and to believe him within the limitlessness of God—these have been suggestive both of profundity concerning himself and of deeper understanding about ourselves.

To move, finally, into the area of observable action—"the works themselves"—may seem to be a concession he was making to the need for greater simplicity. A man is known, we say, by what he does. A good tree brings forth good fruit; an evil tree, evil fruit. This is a fairly workable rule of thumb and although it is not the whole story, we feel reasonably sure of judgments based on it. This is the logic of work. It is certainly less suspect than its opposite index which says that any cause-and-effect relation between human nature and human conduct is illusory.

Jesus had a great deal to say about his work, so much, in fact, that our three previous studies[1] in his self-identification have indicated much deeper and less frequently probed levels than he usually shared with his friends. Observe what is reported in an earlier context:

[1] *"The Logic of Belief," "The Logic of Sight," "The Logic of Identity."*

23

The Jews took up stones again to stone him. Jesus answered them, "I have shown you many good works from the Father; for which of these do you stone me?" The Jews answered him, "We stone you for no good work but for blasphemy; because you, being a man, make yourself God." Jesus answered them, "Is it not written in your law, 'I said, you are gods'? If he called them gods to whom the word of God came (and scripture cannot be broken), do you say of him whom the Father consecrated and sent into the world, 'You are blaspheming,' because I said, 'I am the Son of God'? If I am not doing the works of my Father, then do not believe me; but if I do them, even though you do not believe me, believe the works, that you may know and understand that the Father is in me and I am in the Father." [John 10:31-38]

(1)

Much of interest is to be found in these words. It would seem that the Jews mentioned in the episode distrusted the maxim that a man is what he does, for they insisted that their violent hostility to Jesus was not against what he did—which they agreed was "good work"—but for what he claimed to be—making himself God. No measure of good works could cancel the "blasphemy" of such a claim.

As if to counter the charge of blasphemy he seems almost to dissociate himself from his work: "Even though you do not believe me, believe the works." There was value in recognizing what he did as important in itself since good work has integrity no matter who does it. But Jesus, simply because he is talking practically and not theoretically—or, as we say, arguing for a decision—adds at once that to believe in the works themselves would be the way through which belief in him as "in the Father" was to come. "Again they tried to arrest him, but he escaped from their hands." If these words are to be taken literally they mean that he was already in "their hands," that there was a struggle, and that he broke loose and escaped. It is not easy for us to see why such tension should have developed over so slight a matter until we realize that Jesus was, by the logic of work, identifying himself with God in such a way as to be thought blasphemous.

(2)

This identification with God was a familiar one. Others had made it. In a culture so God-oriented as was Israel's it was no mark of special piety or endowment to assign to one's efforts a motive and a will beyond oneself. "Rabbi," said Nicodemous, "we know that you are a teacher come from God; for no one can do these signs that you do, unless God is with him" (John 3:2). This can hardly be thought a unique tribute; "no one can do these signs" indicates that many did them and that they invariably identified the doer as a companion of God. And the way the record represents Jesus as ignoring the remark in his concern to press on to the necessity of being born anew, would seem to support this.

There are two components to this identification. The first is represented by his word: "The works that I do in my Father's name, they bear witness to me" (John 10:25). To put this in language more familiar to us he is saying: I am the Father's agent; I work in my Father's name, and the credentials of my agency are the works themselves. What I do accredits me to Him. In other words, if you want to identify me, observe what I do. This is the general rule of thumb that says a man is what he does.

There is more to it than that: the reason for observing—and believing—his works is not simply to assign to them the proper motive and power. "Believe the works, that you may know and understand that the Father is in me and I am in the Father"

(John 10:38). Here agency moves over to identity, to the in-ness that we have spoken of earlier, and reminds us again of the confidence expressed by Paul and directed toward his friends in Philippi: "God is at work in you, both to will and to work his good pleasure."

(3)

If we are diffident about venturing into the self-consciousness of Jesus except as his recorded words give us warrant, we need not hesitate to venture into his sense of vocation. So familiar is this confidence that it needs no detailed comment here. From his first-recorded word in the Temple, spoken to his frightened mother, to his final commitment of himself in Gethsemane and on Calvary, he was consciously and resolutely dedicated to his Father's business. "And he who sent me is with me; he has not left me alone, for I always do what is pleasing to him" (John 8:29-30). The record continues: "As he spoke thus, many believed in him."

In the light of this it strikes us as strange that during his last mortal days he had to confront the Inner Circle with the logic of works. What "many believed" had to be reaffirmed to them. On even so matter-of-fact a level, it was not easy for them to understand. Why?

Perhaps we can find an answer to this difficulty by looking momentarily at ourselves. The logic of works is the basis of a philosophical system called Pragmatism. It says: whatever works is true. This certifies an idea or a process as credible in terms of its workability. Thus the idea, honesty is the best policy, is true only so long as it is the best. Existentialism is a modern deviant of this idea. It says: only the immediately existent or uncomplicated state of consciousness has validity.

It is interesting, we think, to note that in the logic of works

Jesus might be said to have been speaking as a pragmatist or an existentialist. This does not pigeonhole him as a first-century advocate of schools of thought made popular in our century. It says, rather, that in these systems the element of validity was used by him to identify himself—pragmatically, existentially.

"Believe me for the sake of the works." How simple; how promising! He had been called an agent of the prince of devils because he cast out devils. His answer was a pragmatic one: what sort of prince of devils would he be that repudiated his own accomplices? The accusation crumpled under the pressure of existential fact.

If, then, he was not working in the name of the prince of devils, what were his auspices? Again his appeal was to the existential fact; his works were the manifestation of Someone who was known by kindness, mercy, patience, pity, forgiveness and so on. Evidence for this was overwhelming; not a single member of the Twelve but could have endlessly documented what he was by the things they had seen him do.

(4)

This suggests two things to us: the first concerns our understanding of him; the second—as in the three previous studies—our understanding of ourselves.

We have said that there are certain so-called metaphysical aspects of the person of Christ which are beyond the comprehension of those who do not oxidize their understanding of things by breathing the pure oxygen of philosophy. Our Lord seems to have felt the necessity of an identification of himself to his closest friends in the dimension of depth, but such evidence as we have points to the fact that they were unequipped for grasping it. They were "slow of heart to believe." The post-resurrection affirmation of Thomas, "My Lord and my God," came when he saw what he thought was a body of flesh, marked by unhealed wounds.

So, when the creeds say "very God of very God, begotten not made," we need a philosopher's help to understand what is meant. This is not the language of ordinary experience; it is opaque to common light. But when the magnificence of complete forgiveness offered to his executioners evoked the centurion's confession: This man was a son of God, we need no explanation. There before us is the inescapable, unimpeachable, existential fact. It is, therefore, something for which we must be grateful, that Jesus allowed his friends to test his divine sonship by the things that he did. Furthermore, we may be sure that most of the myriads who have loved him have had no other reason than "the works themselves." To them the ultimate credential is: "He went about doing good."

The second suggestion concerns an understanding of ourselves. This is an emphasis that has been made in each of the foregoing three studies. It can take nothing from the grandeur of Christ to see in his understanding of himself a clue to man's proper self-understanding. Indeed that this is a part of his own intention is clear from the record. "By your fruits you shall know them," he said, and he must have said it often. "Out of the heart are the issues of life," and this refers to the practical things men do. And in the memorable picture of the Last Judgment, those who are assigned to endless joy are those who have done works of mercy and love for the little ones of earth. In other words, they were identified by "the works themselves."

Most startling, however, of all that he promised his friends during the fateful last days of his life was the assurance that they were to do "greater works" when and because he had gone to his Father. This is something we cannot say has come about. Where is he who dares to say that he is the fulfillment of that promise? But there is a way in which we can appropriate it

qualitatively: in our sophisticated age, the most easily understood evidence of God is not found in the logic of belief, of
sight or of identity, but in the logic of work.

(5)

We have not yet answered the question as to why, when so
many had believed because of his works, it was necessary for
Jesus to reassert the logic of works to his most intimate friends.
Two things may be said: He had always been more or less of an
enigma to them, as indeed he has been down the centuries. It is
a persistent habit of the human mind to seek answers to puz-
zles in terms that are themselves obscure. Only once in the
record do we see this; it is the famous confession of Peter: "To
whom shall we go? You have the words of eternal life; and we
have believed and have come to know, that you are the Holy
One of God" (John 6:68-69). That was identification in depth.
It may be taken as a flash illumination of what went on more
often than the record seems to indicate. Unhappily, we must
agree that it did not do very much for the man who, in a spate
of exuberance, formulated it. Within a very few days he had
repudiated it with an oath.

The second thing is that having met this deeper quest for
understanding that animated his bewildered friends, Jesus returned to the level where comprehension was easy, where doubt
was hard. For on the existential level not only Jesus, but his
friends as well, were to be identified with the Father who was
in him. And yet we must admit that this does not dispel the
element of mystery that infuses man's identification with God,
not through metaphysics but through work. Even the logic of
work must be seen within the dimension of depth.

It is summed up in a profound word of the great apostle:

From now on, therefore, we regard no one from a human point of view; even though we once regarded Christ from a human point of view, we regard him thus no longer. Therefore, if any one is in Christ, he is a new creation; the old has passed away, behold, the new has come. All this is from God, who through Christ reconciled us to himself and gave us the ministry of reconciliation; that is, God was in Christ reconciling the world to himself . . . and entrusting to us the message of reconciliation. [II Cor. 5:16-19]

DISCIPLESHIP SEEN

IN THE DIMENSION

OF DEPTH

Part II

5 THE ENTHUSIAST

I will follow you wherever you go. LUKE 9:57

If our Lord was concerned that his friend should understand him within the dimension of depth and if, in so speaking about himself, he also made it possible for them to understand themselves in deeper terms, it is to be expected that the relation they sustained to him—discipleship—would, in the process, take on gravity.

Jesus inherited something of the popularity that John the Baptist had stimulated in the Jordan valley, but it was necessary for him to give it a character of his own. The fear of doom —the wrath to come—that sent scribe and soldier, Pharisee and publican, crowding to the thundering desert preacher was not the message John's more powerful successor brought. John had warned of ruin, Jesus spoke of good news; John foretold disaster, Jesus offered what must have sounded like security. But it was anything but sentimental optimism.

We must allow for the certainty that both disaster and security were misunderstood by many or understood in shallow terms. Except neurotic fear which rises from hidden recesses of the soul, fear is for the most part a shoal on which the mind is marooned for a moment but from which it can quickly move into deep, navigable water. And similarly a sense of security, more often than not, is an illusion that can as quickly be dispelled as created. This is why mass movements, no matter whether their focus be political, religious or whatever do not very long survive the shock or the sedative that activates them.

(1)

On his last journey south, as Jesus moved toward Jerusalem there was evidence of growing disaffection within the group. They were quarreling about greatness, each one, we may imagine, laying claim to distinction for reasons less than convincing to the others. This grasping self-esteem indicates a pathetic shallowness of understanding of their role as disciples. It furthermore discloses their subtly growing feeling of insecurity. Why else does one boast about one's superior right to the security that greatness is mistakenly thought to guarantee?

They had just passed through Samaria where they had expected and encountered hostility. Add to that the senseless bickering of the disciples that Jesus overheard and which he had rebuked with the famous maxim: "If any one would be first, he must be last of all and servant of all" (Mark 9:35). In such circumstances one would have thought that the unconditional offer of the nameless enthusiast whose words provide our text would have evoked from the Master a similarly enthusiastic acceptance. To his surprise, no doubt, he got exactly the opposite.

"Wherever you go"—the words that shaped his promise— sounded like a long journey; to us it represents the ultimate in commitment. Numberless young persons have similarly responded to the necessity for dedication. One remembers the gospel hymn which has given voice to many a responding heart:

> I'll go where you want me to go, dear Lord;
> I'll be what you want me to be.

Now we do not need to make much of the fact that this extravagant offer was unsolicited. Jesus had not invited him to share his journey for even so much as a furlong. And we may, if we wish, dismiss him as no more than a fellow pilgrim in the nondescript hordes that were making their way to the Holy City, one who, in the holiday mood, would with little restraint abandon himself to almost any enterprise.

The reason for the rebuff he got—and it was hardly less than that—must be found in an insight of Jesus which is only hinted at in the reply he gave the man. "Foxes have holes, and birds of the air have nests; but the Son of man has nowhere to lay his head" (Luke 9:58). What does this mean? Simply that what seems to be security in the natural creation—holes and nests—is not possible for the Son of Man. This, we think, does not mean that Jesus was merely describing himself as a homeless vagabond. He had a home. It means, in solemn truth, that none of the sons of man can be secure. Nowhere to lay his head; that is the perfect metaphor for picturing the essential and irremediable insecurity within which human life must be lived.[1]

(2)

Here was a man who, at least for the duration of his enthusiasm, was reaching out for security in the future. Perhaps in

---

[1] Cf. the leading article in *Saturday Review*, Aug. 20, 1955, entitled "The Way to be Safe Is Never to be Secure," by Charles P. Curtis. The topic is a quotation from Benjamin Franklin.

the festive mood that excited the hearts of the multitudes of his fellow pilgrims he felt a sense of belonging to something that was gay, substantial, protective. This was a bulwark against the constant threat of enemy overlords the sight of whom chilled the native Galilean heart with fear and heated it with rage. The way ahead, both for his subjugated nation and for his own private fortunes, was precarious. At last, in a quite unanticipated way, he found himself in the presence of one of those rare individuals who are themselves so vital that they seem to radiate assurance wherever they go. What was more natural than that he should volunteer to follow Jesus wherever he would go? "Wherever" meant the unmeasured miles and the unforeseen encounters which would daunt a solitary traveler but which, in such company, would turn themselves into the welcome actualities of security.

It must have been what we today call naïve confidence that our Lord heard in these hearty words. He could, of course, have put him to the test. They had not long since left the sullen Samaritans who jeered at passing Jerusalem worshipers. Was this man willing to go back where the Samaritans lived? Once, many months before, Jesus had invited two men whom he had selected as followers to go with him and see where he lived. Would the enthusiast be willing to go back to the undistinguished village where Jesus had never been understood or secure? There were many "places" forward and backward in time, in the "wherever" of this volunteer, to which Jesus might have pointed. Instead he responded with the somber words that took from him any prospect of a place to lay his head. The wild creatures were better off wherever they went because security is never their concern.

We do not overlook the possibility that Jesus' words were spoken as much to himself as to the pilgrim who in that famous moment drew alongside and offered his companionship. Jesus was aware of his insecurity; the reasons for it abounded among both friends and adversaries and he might well be indulged a despondent forecast of his future. Nevertheless, the fact of man's basic insecurity is now, as it was then, something to which most of us refuse to accommodate ourselves. We all tend to think that under the proper auspices, security lies just beyond and beckons us with its promise. Was Jesus' response to this man a rebuke to this insatiable longing that none of us willingly relinquishes and never realizes?

(3)

It is not pessimism that prompts this reflection. To say human life is insecure does not say that it is fated to futility. He would be less than a man in more ways than one who, if he could, would exchange the hazards of the human struggle for a secure nest or a snug burrow. It is the very fact of insecurity that gives life something of its zest. To those who understand life in its proper dimensions even the certainty of dying—which would seem to be the ultimate cancellation of one's hopes for security—is not regarded as defeat. There is no hiding place, there is no sanctuary, there is no hole, no nest, no fortress impregnable. "Wherever" we go we encounter the jeopardy into which life has initiated us. The son of man still has nowhere to lay his head.

We may try to escape this sense of hazard by saying that everybody knows that moth and rust and thief threaten the things on which we depend for our security. The risk may be worth it but the loser should not whimper. If he catches the thief he will punish him but not without a touch of sympathy. Is he not also seeking security? But in the loftier realms of the spirit we say man can be secure. Is there not treasure in heaven? This has so long been a pious way of talking about ourselves that it seems impious to question it. And yet if we speak of heavenly treasure—meaning the intangibles that we can fleetingly claim as our own—we must be prepared to accept their elusiveness also.

Consider, for example, the pursuit of wisdom, the quest for an intellectual security against which the gates of dubiety cannot prevail. All men to whom the mind's restless voyaging is the highest adventure seek a haven for their ultimate mooring. And yet it is never found. The paradox of intellectual progress is that the more one knows the more one senses the limitations of knowing. Not only are there limits within man's intellectual endowment, they are in the nature of the knowable. The illusion of scientism lies just here. When the formula that can integrate the twin facts of gravitation and electromagnetism is finally established—Einstein said he had it but could not prove it experimentally or explain it fully with the mathematical vocabulary he had—the phenomena of the universe will not be packaged and the universe secure within a tight equation closed to further inquiry. Those who offer their minds to go "wherever" in the expectation that all the answers are waiting such commitment must be told that the mind of the Son of Man has no place to lay its head.

This does not say that we know nothing with finality. There are great bases of fact that are like the famous basalt hexagonal pillars of the Giant's Causeway on the north coast of Ireland. These solid columns form a high promontory leading into the sea for two hundred yards. Out beyond the point where one can stand in safety there is visible, in the rise and fall of the sea, a continuation of the solid bastion, until it is finally lost in the foaming waters. One does not abandon the use of the mind because it cannot bridge the sea; to do that is infidelity to the Spirit of Truth. But no matter what the area of human inquiry, we must not think that our natural faculties will take us "wherever."

What of other aspects of the human quest? Are those who hunger and thirst for righteousness' sake not to be filled? We cannot be sure. Certain it is that those who have feasted and drunk most fully of righteousness are less sure they are full than those whose spiritual quest has been little more than occasional nibbling. There is a blessedness in hunger and thirst; they are evidence of normal function. But that the known future can hold the security of spiritual repletion is a delusion, not a promise. And this derives from the very nature of the human spirit. It is the saint who knows this most certainly. "Not that I have already obtained this or am already perfect; but I press on . . ." (Phil. 3:12).

(4)

Finally, the inner contradiction that in our land bedevils the pursuit of physical or material security is apparent to most. It seems to be keenest in a society that has the highest standard of living the world has ever known, and since there is no statistical optimum point at which security exists, the more things we have the more we have to lose and the less secure we feel. "Blessed are the poor," not because there is beatitude in penury but because the relative successes of the effort to survive are less productive of fear and rage than the absolute frustrations of the rich man's demands for security. The "wherever" of physical security leads to no indestructible nest and to no "fall-out" proof cellar.

Our concern, however, returns finally to the happy pilgrim who made his bid for discipleship on the security hypothesis. We do not know what happened to him though it is not difficult to surmise. How many do we know who still respond to the Christian testimony because they think it offers measurable protection now and the sanctuary of heaven at last? Jesus is called Savior, never Protector. He who was to save his people from their sins said that he who saves his life loses it. When he said that the rich man's wealth could not guarantee him the security of the kingdom, his friends asked in dismay: "Who then can be saved?" (Matt. 19:25). And the answer, given in another connection, was: "He who endures to the end" (Matt. 10:22). Jesus spoke rarely about being saved, never about being safe. How odd the perversion of the role of discipleship that it is thought of almost exclusively in terms of a privileged status in a precarious world, now and hereafter. This is shallowness. The "wherever" of Jesus opened a vista so splendid and terrible, so deep and measureless, that the feckless enthusiasms of men dissipate like cloud wisps in its vastness. "If any man would come after me, let him deny himself . . . and follow me" (Matt. 16:24). What's that? Deny? Yes: and still the Son of Man has nowhere to lay his head and few to share his pillowless pilgrimage.

6 THE CONSCRIPT

To another he said, "Follow me." But he said, "Lord, let me first go and bury my father." But he said to him, "Leave the dead to bury their own dead; but as for you, go and proclaim the kingdom of God. LUKE 9:59-60

This man was no volunteer, no enthusiast with a fondness for spacious-sounding words like "wherever." He may have heard the brief exchange between Jesus and the other man and noted, with some dismay, the preferred status that foxes and birds were said to have in this uncertain world. To go along with the Galilean was poor insurance; perhaps there was greater safety in the opposite direction.

(1)

The study of history is the most important of intellectual disciplines. Here the Son of Man has a clear advantage over the foxes and birds, an advantage which has often compensated somewhat for his lack of a place to lay his head. The animal's built-in repository of experience will take him back to last year's nest or burrow—if he is a perennial nester or burrower and, if his enterprise demands new quarters annually, to the general area where homesites are congenial. This is the way nature creates history for creatures whose memories are no more than a tool of the survival instinct. But the study of history is something of graver importance to the Son of Man. The tangled episodes of the past must be disengaged in order that the living energies that animated them may be exposed and understood. To study the Revolutionary War is to identify, not only individuals and events, but the giant energies that thrust a pioneer people toward the establishment of a free society. To know this is to be able to conserve and step up these energies if it is important to keep society free. Compared with nest-building and hole-digging, history-making is the task of giants. This means making history not in the sense of making destiny but in making clear time's linear perspectives to those whose myopia foreshortens time and distorts space.

To know history is to know all; it is the base on which all sequence rests from digit to doomsday, for without sequence order is meaningless. There is little wonder, therefore, that man is a record-leaving animal. One individual's memory adjoined to another's and his to another's probes backward along the way individual, tribe, nation and culture have come. It is like the rear-view mirror by which one sees the withdrawing highway while moving forward along the welcoming road. "Civilization," says Dr. Vannever Bush, "proceeds because man can store, transmit, and consult the record." [1]

For this reason—the importance and the fascination—the past can easily become a drug to depress or excite so that the present seems forbidding or frenzied. How easy then to use the faculty of memory as a defense against the now; to lose existential responsibility in nostalgia. Thus subtly the past becomes a delusion; history a deceiver.

(2)

This was the trouble with the man in our text. Not, perhaps, in such heroic proportions as we have described; but it seems clear that his quest for security, unlike that of the enthu-

---

[1] "For Man to Know," in *Atlantic Monthly*, August, 1955.

siast, was to be found by a retreat into the past. But, as we shall see, if there is no security in the future for the Son of Man, there is less in the past. Such nests and holes as are to be found belong to last year's occupants and are already abandoned. There is no reason for thinking that this man wanted to go back to recover the dynamics of progress and it is on some such understanding of his motives that the sharp rebuke of Jesus is defensible.

"Lord, let me first go and bury my father"; this would seem to be an innocent request. And yet it could hardly have been so. The ritual of mourning was not simple; it was sustained and costly. Jeremiah, the prophet who more than any other interpreted the great and tragic events of his time in terms of the dynamic action of the Almighty in history, also had a strange preoccupation with funerals and encouraged their elaboration. His influence still strongly persisted so that at the time of Jesus a loyal son whose father was dead and unburied would most certainly not have been on his way to Jerusalem to spend the holidays.

Jesus' invitation was crisp and peremptory. "Follow me"; and the man's response was equally so. Except that Jesus seems to have detected something of dishonesty, dishonesty that deserved rebuke. The exposure of the man's insincerity is seen in the sardonic suggestion of the Master which, if taken literally, is quite absurd. Dead people do not bury their dead; they have no dead. What a ghoulish picture one can conjure up in these terms; the lifeless body brought to burying ground and summarily abandoned by the sorrowing kinfolk. Then the ominous silence and the noiseless motion of spectral figures, bending to carry the newcomer away, first to swathe it in spices and the cerements of death and then to assign it to a solitary grave. The dead burying the dead!

Efforts have been made to soften the apparent heartlessness

of Jesus in the presence of this man's alleged sorrow. This is unnecessary when we realize that there was no sorrow there. The man simply saw discipleship as an option that offered little until the past was conciliated. For this reason we are to understand the rebuke of Jesus as metaphor. It was not a nonsensical proposal that dead men should bury dead men, nor was it a blunt disparagement of the filial obligation. What exactly was he confronting here?

(3)

It is fairly obvious that he was dealing with that state of mind that acknowledges the necessity of living in the present but finds its satisfactions in living in the past. The man in our story falsely pays respect—that he does not feel—to a past—that he does not have. Jesus says metaphorically: Dead issues are for dead minds! If man cannot count on a nest and a burrow for his future security, neither can he count on corpses.

This does not settle the problem that our faculty of memory creates. We have said that without an awareness of history—which is orderly recollection—we can have no awareness of order, and that would mean no vital awareness of God, which provides us with our ground of faith in history's meaning. That "the past is prologue" must not be allowed to mean that it is a sanctuary for the timid and the lazy.

The metaphor Jesus used indicates his awareness that history is alive and presents new issues as it grows. It follows that the living mind exhibits its vitality by the way it welcomes and deals with new issues.

Of course, in the years when our Lord's ministry was begun there was a widely accepted gravitation toward the past. To the faithful son of Israel, the present became increasingly intolerable. Indeed to live vividly in the present was a sort of apostasy to the former glories, both real and fable, of the Chosen

People. We cannot feel the shock that shook those who heard Jesus say that the Temple was to be utterly destroyed. What he should have said was that the Temple was indestructible because in the past it had been the sanctuary of both God and His faithful ones. The silver lining to the heavy cloud that mantled Palestine was seen only by those who looked backward over their shoulders.

Jesus himself was emancipated from the past's bondage. One of the remarkable aspects of his public utterances is their lack of chauvinism. He did not need to retell the epic tales of his people in order to win a following. This both puzzled and angered his hearers. "Are you greater than our father Abraham, who died? And the prophets died! Who do you claim to be?" (John 8:53). This may have been honest bewilderment. But when he said, "If you were Abraham's children, you would do what Abraham did" (John 8:39), they "took up stones to throw at him." What was it that Abraham had done? He had made as radical a break with the past as is conceivable; he left country, kindred and his father's house to go into an unknown world.

This was the sort of radical break that Jesus had also made; country, kindred and his Father's house were left behind when he ventured forth with the startling announcement that the kingdom of heaven was at hand. Not the throne of David, but the kingdom of heaven, which had never yet been.

(4)

It is not difficult to see why Jesus, confronted by this wish to escape the present by retreat to the past in one who was called to become a disciple, should address himself to it so sharply. This was part of the problem of the Pharisee and the scribe. Professor Hocking speaks somewhere of this state of mind as that of "Lot's wife, congealed in an attitude of retrospect." For this hapless woman there was mesmeric fascination in the sight of her past even while it was perishing in flaming bitumen.

To have warned against this danger was hardly enough. There was no security back home among the dead, nor, for that matter, among the living who so far as we know might have been similarly preoccupied with the lifeless past. It was necessary for Jesus to make a positive suggestion to the man he had rebuked. This he did in memorable words: "As for you, go and proclaim the kingdom of God."

The point has often been made that Jesus did not leave the man with his easy excuse. He might have been dismissed as undesirable material for discipleship. What we have not seen so clearly is the fact that our Lord's invitation was put in the command "follow me"; but his orders, once he had punctured the man's preoccupation with the past, was "go." We must be careful not to make too much of this, remembering that the dead burying the dead was the language of metaphor describing a state of mind. Nevertheless, what is better calculated to correct the antiquarian mood than responsibility for something that is imminent? The metaphor may be enlarged to contain more than rebuke. There are dead to be buried and the dead will take care of that. What you can do, however, while you witness this weird operation, is to startle the gravediggers with a shout announcing that the kingdom of God is coming. Imagine what is to happen when the kingdom of life challenges the kingdom of death!

This is the point in human experience where another motivation is joined to memory if one is to delve deeply into life. Again let Dr. Bush[2] say it for us:

> . . . curiosity—that strange characteristic of man which, more than anything else, has led to his ascendance on our planet, and which

[2] *Op. cit.*, p. 40.

drives him still toward the mastery of what may now seem the unknowable. . . . Many scientists derive their strongest motivation from
religion and carry on their mission by faith.

The conscript who refused to be decoyed from the certainties
of the past—and what is less ambiguous than death?—should
remind us of the pitfall that besets many of the "back to" movements for which our support is daily solicited. Where do we
not encounter them? In politics, economics, education, diplo-
macy, theology—everywhere, it seems, except perhaps in tech-
nology and entertainment. This is explained by some as evidence that life runs in ever-recurring cycles and that whether
we want it or not, we are endlessly going back to something
we thought we had left forever.

Even assuming that this accurately presents life there should
be no peril in such an attitude unless it represents a conscious
satisfaction on our part, in escaping the present, in consorting
with the dead instead of proclaiming the kingdom of the living.
No matter where we encounter this it is evidence of spiritual
exhaustion.

It is our contention here that Jesus, during the last fateful
days of his earthly ministry, felt the necessity of presenting the
role of discipleship in depth. It was not easy with those for
whom life was primarily a quest for security—in the future or
in the past. Religion today suffers much from this sort of understanding of its place in culture. So long as it provides a way of
escape from the exigent demands of the now, it is a spurious
and bloodless thing.

What happened to this conscript? We can only guess; he
went back to the charnel house; the others moved on toward
Jerusalem without him.

John Greenleaf Whittier, a Quaker poet little read in these
times, concludes "Snow-Bound," a long poem of reflections

written during a New England winter, with a tolerant yet pointed rebuke to the mood we have been considering:

> Clasp, Angel of the backward look
> The brazen covers of thy book.

And then, stout activist that he was, resentful of the imprisoning weather, he is happy to be able to say:

> E'en while I look, I can but heed
> The restless sands' incessant fall,
> Importunate hours that hours succeed
> Each clamorous with its own sharp need,
> And duty keeping pace with all.

Our conscript, bemused by the "Angel of the backward look," could not see "the restless sands' incessant fall" and so neither followed the Master nor went to proclaim the kingdom.

7 THE UNDECIDED

> Another said, "I will follow you, Lord; but let me first say fare-well to those at my home." Jesus said to him, "No one who puts his hand to the plow and looks back is fit for the kingdom of God.
> LUKE 9:61-62

Our concern is to understand the meaning of discipleship within the dimension of depth in which Jesus set it during his last mortal days. And we have seen that man's quest for security, never realized because of the nature of experience and never relinquished because of the nature of spirit, can satisfy the demands of discipleship only on superficial levels. Assuring oneself of security in the future tends to desensitize one's response to the present, as does also his retreat into the past from the pressures of the exigent moment. We cannot clasp the "insubstantial pageant" of our dreams as Shakespeare phrased it, or "pillage the past" as Lewis Mumford puts it. We must, in the language of the record, "go and proclaim the kingdom of God," let security fall where it may.

(1)

It is interesting to note that in the account Matthew gives of this episode there are only two men involved besides Jesus. One of them, the Enthusiast as we have called him, was a scribe. Perhaps the unpromising future to which most scribes had to look forward was part of the reason for his "wherever" commitment. The other was a disciple. This is hardly to be understood except in general terms since it is unlikely that one of the Twelve who had already been with him for many months suddenly realized that he had forgotten to say good-by to the folks.

Or is it, on the contrary, to be taken to indicate that this disciple saw destiny riding with the holiday crowds; that he felt he would not likely survive the storm that was so soon to break and that the farewell he wished to speak to those at home was the leave-taking of a doomed man? This would be seeing discipleship in depth and readiness to accept it. Nevertheless, we dismiss this as implausible for the reason that Jesus, in another direct word, spoke of the unfitness of suchlike backward-lookers for the enterprise on which they were already embarked.

There is, however, in this man's problem an element of pathos that in Luke's account did not concern the other two. The Enthusiast could make up his mind for insufficient reasons and though momentarily he was rebuffed by Jesus' warning, his was the sort of temperament that could bounce back and bounce away in another direction with little loss of momentum. The Conscript could not make the necessary response because he was moored to the past and to cast off from that loyalty was, he thought, to lose all anchorage. Even the new chart and compass of the kingdom of God would have set him forth on a journey he had no heart to undertake.

The Undecided affects our interest in quite a different fashion. He was neither footloose nor bound as the other two, he was caught in a tension between two interests both of which were good. For this reason the melancholy judgment of Jesus, "not fit," has particular poignancy.

The reason we think this man an equivocator is that he is described as already having "put his hand to the plow." We do not need to bother with the orientalisms with which some commentators have thrown light on this exchange. We know the

Palestinian farmer plowed with one hand and that a furrow is not likely to run straight if the plowman looks back over his shoulder. These are human foibles, as likely to be seen in a Georgia share-cropper as in a Galilean farmer. Or, it might be added, as prevalent in bankers and politicians as in the less pretentious tillers of the soil.

(2)

This man found himself in the position made clear by the difference between the connective conjunction *and* and the adversitive conjunction *but*. It is part of the moral climate of our times to see all conjunctions as corelative. Because every situation is contingent, ambiguous and ambivalent, we are told that, when confronted by the necessity for choice, we should rarely if every say *either-or* but rather *both-and*.

Consider this man's predicament. We do not think, customarily, that one's family is the opposite of one's Christian vocational responsibility. When our Lord spoke of divisions within families because of him, he was describing neither a normal nor a desirable state of affairs. He was not indifferent to the family bond. Whatever the sense of bereavement that pressed on his spirit the day he left a simple home in Nazareth and went out, never again to be known as the son of Mary but henceforth as the Son of Man, is not disclosed to us. But we cannot think that he, who had said farewell to his family and invested his leave-taking with more than simple amenity, could have thought that this person who felt the family tug was about to yield to something sinister.

Add to the essential nobility of family solidarity, which is not carelessly regarded, the element of legitimate caution exhibited by this man. To safeguard action against imprudence is to protect oneself from rashness or haste and is the quality that inspires trust in others. The cautious man makes the good executive though he will hardly lead a crusade.

And yet the caution that is the ally of prudence can easily become the indecision that is the ally of inaction. Indecision is arrested caution and easily hardens into formalism. It will say, with plausible assurance, that the time for action is unpropitious—which it is; or that the consequences of action are unpredictable—which they are. Thus the intention of caution to hold on to momentary security until extended security is promised results in the calcification of the will. What the man should have said was, "I will follow you, Lord, *and* say good-by to those that are at home." The words "but first," seen against the dimension of depth, expose the thinness of his proposed dedication.

(3)

We lack no sympathy for this man. In a real way he is Everydisciple. Life is so complex that loyalties are never single or simple. Only in the matter of ultimates are they exclusive, such as, for example, our belief in the primacy of love over hate. And even here we encounter the ambivalence that shakes self-confidence to its center. We catch ourselves every so often exercising a certain type of love that is little more than the weapon of a certain kind of hostility. The problem—never to be so neatly solved as to allow us to write *finis* after it—is to find one encompassing loyalty that can touch both the zenith and the nadir of human commitment. This is rarely done and when it is, it will, paradoxically, exhibit the element of tragedy as well as of triumph.

Consider the cases of General Robert E. Lee and Dr. Albert Schweitzer as illustrative of this problem. Lee was a tragic hero and the tragic element arose from the choice he felt compelled to make for what appears to us as the lesser of two noble loyalties. Few pictures are more affecting in retrospect than this profoundly conscientious and gifted man, choosing to lead in a cause in which he truly believed but could not wholly believe, and leading it to its agonizing end. Lee's descent into failure was both stoical and Christian in that with complete disregard of personal fortune and with deep Christian piety he shared in the unnecessary ruin of something to which a deep loyalty compelled him. And yet the verdict of history is not sentimental when it understands him as both pathetic and splendid because of his foredoomed effort to deal with exclusive circles of loyalties within the circumference of a deep religious faith. As he looked from Arlington across the river that separated North and South he might have said, "Union, I will follow you, but first let me settle the problem of the sovereign rights of the State." That was, at that moment in Lee's experience, tragedy.

Schweitzer shows the problem in a way that only within recent years has won reluctant praise from a cynical world. Here again there is the sweeping circumference of the God-dedicated life within which are found the lesser orbits of other high loyalties. That he is what is loosely described as a genius settles nothing. To be a master in the realms of music, theology and philosophy was an aim he brilliantly attained. To be a master of the healing art invited and won his successful pursuit. And then? The wretched, black sufferers in Africa's equatorial forest called on him to atone for the neglect and exploitation they had suffered for three centuries at the hands of their white brethren. His was the choice between the greater of two loyalties. One might ask whether as he looks across the Ogowe river that divides the jungle from the hospital at Lambaréné he has ever said: "Art and philosophy, I choose you, and let me first heal the black folk of the forest." That, at that moment in Schweitzer's experience, was triumph.

The point to remember here is that while Civil War general

and *le grand docteur* settled loyalties within the larger loyalty, one is a tragic, the other a triumphant, figure. Why is it that the man in our story was not able to do this?

(4)

The word "fit" is itself interesting. *Euthetos* means "well placed"; it represents a factual rather than a moral judgment. Not to be well placed is to be out of line, causing disorder and awkwardness instead of precision and grace. This is a concept that is relevant to every aspect of human experience and lends itself easily to everything from mathematics to delinquency.

It is familiar in the line of scrimmage, the foul line, the base line, and in the penalties that are inflicted—offsides, out-of-bounds, footfault—to those who get out of line. The musical instrument that is off pitch, the scales that are out of balance, the spirit level that dips ever so slightly off the horizontal, the deviationist of whatever sort and for whatever reason—these are not *euthetos,* they are out of line.

To what extent moral attitudes are involved in this sort of thing must be understood in terms of each particular instance. Specifically, however, in the case of our Equivocator the matter is clear. There was, we assume, no moral culpability involved. He, like the plowman with the reverted eye, could not stay in line and the effort to keep his hand operating in one direction and his eye in another unfitted him to be either a farmer or a surveyor. His awkward antics were pathetic to some, amusing to others, but to all who saw them they represented the futility of indecision.

Jesus saw a good deal of this equivocation. He spoke of salt that was insipid, of light that was darkness. In the last days of his life he saw warm hearts growing cold, bold spirits growing furtive in the presence of mounting suspicion, dedicated hands clutching desperately at a plowhandle and plowing a devious furrow. This ambiguity was to issue, within a few frightening days, in the obscene denial of his most vociferous friend and in the noise of hurrying feet, disappearing in the shadows of an olive orchard as "they all forsook him and fled."

It should be obvious, then, that if we have been able to avoid being put in the categories of the Enthusiast or the Conscript, we shall not easily escape being Undecideds. Is there not, we ask, abundance of justification for refusing to be bound to just one commitment? Life does not run on a one-track loyalty. Anyone half alive has more than one furrow to plow and the fields where we plow may be widely separated. And so we make a virtue of the necessity of indecision, we nurture the satisfactions of the existential response, we even boast of our skill at juggling so many bright balls of purpose in the air. We call it versatility.

And we are not evil withal; we are indeed quite respectable and our urbane multiresponse to life's pressures wins for us other pleasant names. Does this mean that in this welter of our many-furrowed lives, the Christian commitment is so shallowly felt that indecision is easy or, to vary the figure, that the constellation of our separate concerns is not found within the galaxy of an all-enveloping devotion to God?

It is a sorry thing to learn about ourselves that for all our pretensions our indecision puts us out of position; that our backward glance unsteadies the plowhandle and deflects its blade; that we are—in seven of the unhappiest of words—"not fit for the kingdom of God."

8 THE BLESSED EYES

Blessed are the eyes which see what you see! For I tell you that many prophets and kings desired to see what you see, and did not see it, and to hear what you hear, and did not hear it. LUKE 10:23-24.

The story of the dispatch of thirty-five pairs of missioners "into every town and place where he himself was about to come" (Luke 10:1) follows immediately upon the rejection of the unfit man. "After this" is the way the new enterprise is introduced and we are unable to say precisely whether this means a time sequence or a consequence. After the failure of three to understand devotion in depth, he appointed seventy and sent them on ahead of him, two by two. Were they better prepared? Had their loyalty been tested? We do not know.

What is clear, however, is that profession of loyalty was set in secondary position to the practice of loyalty. And it was practice of discipleship in depth. There is something almost peremptory in the way the record represents Jesus as turning from the three to the seventy, as if the occasion was past for arguing the pros and cons of following him. The concerns of the "wherever" Enthusiast for security in the future, of the Conscript for security in the past, and for the Undecided for that sense of security that comes, oddly, in the acceptance of insecurity are dismissed for something so tremendous that it is described as that which kings and prophets had longed to see, but had never seen.

(1)

What is it kings and prophets want? The king, in the experience of Israel, was the spokesman of God in the civil and political realms. All kings, if they deserve the throne at all, want political and civil security; Israel differed in that the king was the agent of God in maintaining it. The king's moral failures were often less serious than his administrative failures. In this way Israel was like neighbor nations. The pagan empire of Rome tolerated the moral impudicities of Nero but an earthquake in Spain and a plague in the capital demanded magisterial skill he could not muster and threatened his rule. Secular power, as exercised by the state, depends on the security of the means of secular survival.

What does the prophet want to see and hear? He, in the experience of Israel, was the spokesman of God in the moral realm. All prophets, if they deserve the role at all, want individual and social righteousness. Their public and private concern is the maintenance of the religious and moral ideals which support civil stability and, for that reason, are the ultimate security of society. The prophets of Israel, both true and false, knew this and presumed upon their right to rebuke the king and the prince. Righteousness alone exalted the nation.

It was at the end of the first report of this multiple effort to announce that the kingdom of God was near, that Jesus privately told the commissioners that they had seen and heard what kings and prophets had desired to see and hear. What was it; the security of a stable state and a righteous citizenry? No; it was something in which the idea and the fact of security seems not to have figured at all. Does this mean that the seventy, apparently chosen at random, may have seen the kingdom testimony and task within a dimension of depth, missed by the three? If so, it should be useful to examine what the chief of their mission said to them as they waited for him to send them out.

(2)

The first note sounded was that of timeliness. "The harvest is plentiful." The emphasis on the bumper opportunity is important. A less confident leader might have said that the picking was sure to be scanty; it had been pretty thoroughly worked over by others, but for those who did not mind hard work and little reward there would be a modest return. Not so, Jesus; the scarcity was not in the field but in the labor supply. "Pray therefore the Lord of the harvest to send out laborers into his harvest" (Luke 10:2). The time and harvest were propitious.

The second note is that of danger. In order to make this vivid it was necessary to abandon the metaphor of harvest and reaper in which peril is reduced to a minimum and employ the metaphor of flock and wolf in which peril is not only heightened to a maximum but in which success is sure to go to the wolves. They were to go out as lambs in the midst of wolves; that meant, to all human seeing, they were going out, not only to fail, but to be destroyed. What of security now?

The third note is that of urgency. Here again the metaphor is changed to a traveler, stripped to the barest economy: no purse, no bag, no sandals, no salute; equipped only with impatience and a benediction: Peace. This was no windy exhortation; it was not blind to the realization that to say "peace" was not to create it; it knew that in some houses and towns the sons of peace would be encountered and in others the sons of strife. But whether one or the other the messenger's own sense of peace would not desert him; with the sons of peace he was to eat and drink as the reward of his labor, to the sons of strife there was to be the simple word of a judgment more appalling than Sodom's but in the face of that doom, the messenger's peace would "return" to him.

In all this we observe that the notion of security is alien to the idea of peace, and yet this peace was not something thought mistakenly to be the aim and the issue of security. What traveler does not make his journey as comfortable as possible by bag, purse, sandal and salute? Are they not designed to give him peace of mind as he travels? To abandon them, we say, is not to become a peace-filled wayfarer but a tramp!

And what more certainly cancels out the possibility of security than "lambs in the midst of wolves"? This is no uneven contest, it is no contest at all. The wolves always win. What then was the point in their venturing forth? To the peace of the lacerated throat and the lifeless carcass? The death wish which we are told is a subconscious retreat from the ravening of life? This would be sheer suicide, man's only escape from terror, man's only expiation for sin! What was there in the announcement "that the kingdom of God has come near" that could give victory to the lambs?

(3)

What happened? It would be interesting to know but the record is reticent. Thirty-five pairs of men going into we do not know how many villages and towns surely had experiences in great variety. We would expect the average number of casualties, spiritual and physical, and perhaps a renegade or two. What we are less prepared to expect is the astonishing announcement on their return that the sheep had won! To be sure, this was not their language; if anything their description was even more dramatic. In the name of their leader demons had been brought into subjection. To which Jesus added his own corroborating word: he too had seen Satan fall like lightning from heaven.

The crusade was not to be called off at that point. To the simple directions with which they had gone out was added plenary authority so sweeping that one hazards the guess that it has never been wholly appropriated. They had gone out without sandals; now they were to tread on serpents and scorpions; they had gone out defenseless—no purse, no bag; now they were strong against "all the power of the enemy"; they had gone out to pursue their solitary and unsaluting way along the road; now nothing was to hurt them. And finally they had been paired off, two names to a team, to find their ways into dangerous places; now they were to rejoice that their names were written, one by one, in heaven on the roll of the heroes.

To say, as we are compelled to say, that this is the language of metaphor, takes nothing from its dimensions. The ecstasy of our Lord as it appears in his vision and his prayer of gratitude demanded language commensurate with his exhilaration of soul. To tread on scorpions and serpents has never been a spiritual discipline except in a few coves in the Smokey mountains, but there has been joy in the subjugation of those demonic impulses that have been, like wolves, devouring sheep. And who, in some moment of spiritual conquest, has not borrowed the words about Satan's headlong plunge from heaven to the abyss, and felt that the phrase correctly described his victory?

(4)

This is what prophets and kings, who wanted to see civil and moral security based on physical and moral invincibility, had never seen. The record says that this was pointed out "privately" to the disciples, meaning, it seems clear, the Twelve. Was this a part of his effort to help them understand discipleship in depth? It is certain, in our times, that we do not expect the sheep to win against the wolves. Is this because we still conceive our devotion to the leader in shallow terms?

Moreover, the word "privately" is interesting in this connection. *Idios,* with a preposition here is thus rendered. It is the direct parent of our word "idiot"; and there are those who say that the idea that the sheep will win over the wolves are talking nonsense.

This is not the place to argue the point. Even those least persuaded of the invincibility of the sheep agree that in numerous places our Lord spoke as if he believed in it, and his was no shallow judgment on the human predicament. He was announced by John in the Jordan Valley as the Lamb that was to take away the world's sin. Why a lamb and not a wolf for this appalling enterprise? It is not enough to see in John's metaphor a reference to a sacrificial ritual common among the Jews. One must go back beyond that and ask what, in the earliest Jewish mind that conceived it, made a lamb instead of some more puissant beast the symbol of victory over sin.

And yet, this notion—the invincibility of the lamb which was disclosed to the blessed eyes—is described today as irrelevant to the world situation. To which the answer must be: it always was irrelevant; and for the reason that the world, in its quest of security, knows the lamb cannot guarantee it. Exactly; and again for the reason that security, in our world, is irrelevant. Only as life is set within dimensions of depth does the paradox of the security of insecurity come into proper focus.

There was a story in *The American Weekly* of November 28, 1954, [1] which told of the son of an assassinated Kenya chief who had led a resistance movement against the Mau Mau. Old tribal customs would have demanded that his son avenge his father's death. But the son David was a Christian who—may

[1] Quoted by Margaret Applegarth in *Moment by Moment.*

we not say it?—saw his commitment to the Way in the dimension of depth. Believing that he could not overcome hate with hate, he and his family moved voluntarily into the barbed wire concentration camp where fifteen hundred Mau Mau fanatics were imprisoned. Kimu, murderer of his father, was among them.

Talk of lambs in the midst of wolves! The story concludes with the amazing fact that today, five hundred of the interned rebels are being trained to go out, a dozen at a time, into other Mau Mau prison camps to teach the redemptive processes by which David won, not only his father's murderer, but also the son of Kenyatta, the imprisoned leader of the whole Mau Mau movement.

After this the Lord appointed seventy others, and sent them . . . two by two . . . as lambs in the midst of wolves . . . [and they] returned with joy, saying, "Lord, even the demons are subject to us in your name.". . . Then turning to the disciples he said privately, "Blessed are the eyes which see what you see!" [Luke 10:1-23]

LIFE'S CRISES SEEN

IN THE DIMENSION

OF DEPTH

Part **III**

9 THE CRISIS OF MORALITY

"If you would be perfect, go, sell what you possess and give to the poor, and you will have treasure in heaven; and come, follow me." When the young man heard this he went away sorrowful; for he had great possessions. MATTHEW 19:21-22

There is another aspect of the dimension of depth to which one is invited by reflection on the last days of our Lord's life. It may be described as the way the determinative experiences of life are probed beneath their familiar and often misleading surfaces. This has already been disclosed by our consideration of Jesus' efforts to help his friends understand him more deeply, and in the ways by which the professed loyalty of some, who intimated an interest in discipleship, was rebuked for its shallowness. In the case of The Blessed Eyes, the uttermost was promised and tested with results that even to our sophistication seem fantastic.

In a manner of speaking every experience is critical, using the word in its primary sense of passing judgment. This is another way of saying every experience is decisive, meaning no more than that it affects a sequence of events. The sequence may be a logical one or quite the opposite. Going to bed logically disposes one to rest; it may, however, dispose one to restlessness. Hence, while every experience is critical, it is not necessarily determinative. We are glad that this is so; otherwise we would be the victims of experience—at least to an intriguing degree—rather than its monitors.

Only when one looks deeply at life does one see its criticalness. To observe that a particular experience is decisive of the next means neither that life, as the comic says, is just one thing after another, nor that one thing certainly determines the next. It means that the existential moment, or mood, or state of consciousness or action exists in its own right and passes judgment on itself. It is essentially critical, not necessarily crucial.

To be sure, this is only one aspect of the matter, the aspect that is stressed by those who call themselves existentialists. However, the critical character of each experience is to be seen not in its isolation from, but in its organic relation to, what precedes and what follows. Life is to be understood as a continuum rather than as a concatenation. Thus, in Wordsworth's famous words:

> Our birth is but a sleep and a forgetting:
> The soul that rises with us, our life's star,
>   Hath elsewhere had its setting,
>   And cometh from afar:
>   Not in entire forgetfulness,
>   And not in utter nakedness
> But trailing clouds of glory do we come
>   From God who is our home.

The utter nakedness of the existential birth is not naked at all; it trails clouds of glory that have swept across immeasurable distances.

(1)

Moral choice illustrates this point. To do or not to do; when faced with the necessity of choosing one or the other, the decision falls and the issue is decided. Not, however, in isolation. Beneath the act lies the substratum of all previous acts and decisions. One cannot, if he wishes to, fracture this moral continuum; what he decides passes judgment on all he has hitherto decided. As no man stands alone insulated from the moral consequence of the acts of his fellows, so no act stands alone. It is simply not true, as we sometimes impatiently say: this is my business and what I do affects no one but me.

There are other areas of experiences besides moral choice that we shall investigate as we consider crisis within the dimension of depth. For the moment our concern is with a man who saw moral responsibility in shallow strata and with the way in which Jesus sought to deal with him.

He is familiarly known as the rich young ruler. As Matthew reports the encounter he is among those who thronged Jesus in the region of Judea beyond the Jordan very shortly before the pilgrims began their descent to Jerusalem. His companions were sick and wanted to be healed, they were puzzled and wanted to be taught. Luke's account of what is a similar if not the same episode places it immediately following the beatitude Jesus had conferred on those eyes that had seen what had been hidden from the eyes of kings and prophets.

The difference in accounts is unimportant for the moral issue involved is the same. It affected the relation of one's moral choice to what in both accounts is called "eternal life." Perhaps, after Jesus' "private" word to the disciples, this man, who had heard the amazing report of the seventy, sought clarification of a problem of his own. He was not offering discipleship to Jesus, but the invincible "peace" with which the missioners had been caparisoned was not his. He was a young man, born to wealth and settled to power, but peace was far from him.

How familiar this is to all of us; one might add to all generations. Youth is a time of turbulence but of the sort that produces its own high-riding satisfactions. Wealth is the guardian of security or can go out and buy it if necessary; and the authority to rule—this is to be embroiled in the responsibilities of administration, of course, but upon them we think there settles the enormous satisfactions of controlling the lives of others. Peace in such terms is not tranquillity, the peace of the placid mind and the untroubled heart. Yet there are not a few who are willing to settle for that kind of peace until something more fully satisfying comes along.

Beyond this, however, was the fact of the man's formal and unsullied rectitude. It may sound smug to modern ears to hear his acknowledgment that he had observed all the commandments, many of which other rich young rulers had flouted. Yet if his claim were true it would have broken a commandment for him to deny it, even for the sake of modesty.

Surely this paragon deserves further examination. If he were telling the truth the moral choices he had made, plus, we assume, the happy circumstances under which he had grown up, should have won for him a sense of moral security commensurate with the security he more or less enjoyed as a man of money and power.

(2)

By all conventional standards of success this man had lived and lived well. Not as a sybarite whose opulent tastes could be satisfied to the uttermost nicety of need and inclination, but as a citizen who felt the sense of responsibility his preferred social position conferred on him. And yet he was not satisfied merely to live; he wanted assurance of life on a higher level—eternal life.

Of course, it is not difficult for the envious to say that having squeezed dry the orange of "life" he was reaching for the new sensations "eternal life" might offer. We are told that the mind of his times had a very hazy idea of what we call immortality, that there was little thought of a sumptuous heaven as our imaginations have pictured it. For this reason it might be argued that his concern was for a guarantee in perpetuity for the life he was already living. This is the problem of security we have already encountered. He had inherited a life of rectitude, wealth and responsibility; how could he inherit an eternal life of the same sort?

The immediate response Jesus made avoided the emphasis on the eternal. When, in answer to the question as to how he had conducted himself, the man replied that he had never killed anybody, he was chaste, respected the property rights of others, was a filial son to father and mother, and—most remarkable of all—had always loved his neighbor as himself, Jesus said that was the way to "enter life." Yet to inherit eternal life required more or something different. What more could one expect? That's exactly what he asked: "What still do I lack?"

We are assuming, of course, that the young ruler was stating his case honestly. Had he been dissembling, we would expect the sort of rebuke that dishonesty always got from Jesus. What we may well ask, however, is how he managed to achieve such a record. If we find the answer to that, we may encounter something important.

The tests that wealth, position and authority make on character are, we are constantly reminded, more exacting than the moral liabilities incurred by poverty, mediocrity and insignificance. In the case of this man victory over good fortune had been achieved. If he was proud of his conquests we shall not blame him overmuch. And yet, when such an achievement is recorded and poverty is not the explanation, how is it to be accounted for? By wealth, indeed.

There was nothing inherently wrong in this man's being in a high financial bracket. Given the inclinations to sobriety and neighborliness, it was easy to exemplify them. Why should not the son of wealthy parents honor his father and mother? Never mind, for the moment, that we know of some who don't; was there not every reason for filial regard toward those who had made life for him so easy? Knowing as we do the causes of murder, why should a rich man kill anyone? And why steal when one already has more than one needs? And why adultery when the externals, at least, of domestic felicity were so congenial? What advantage is dishonesty to one who can afford to tell the truth? The snob is the man who has an inner sense of inferiority. To one who was obviously superior, the love of one's neighbor was at least a sign of self-confidence if nothing else.

(3)

The point of this record is that in the observance of moral rules there was no real contest. It was easy to behave. We do not generalize on this because we dare not. No illusion is more deceptive than that if we were rich and secure we could, with little effort, be good. We are dealing only with this highly exceptional case. And we must be careful to remember that Jesus did not generalize. When he told the man to sell all he had and give it to the poor and become a practicing pauper, he was not setting this up as a moral obligation to mass self-impoverishment.

"If you would be perfect"; this was the condition on which the rich young ruler was to divest himself of wealth and power.

And it turned out that he did not want to be perfect. He was not good enough to want that. Why? Because that was the point at which he was morally vulnerable. He could handle wine, wife and song and get on well with his neighbor. No problem there. But wealth? That was his master; he was the slave of his satisfactions in ordering the lives of others. His moral problem was crucial at that point and when Jesus proposed that it be tackled in the interest of eternal life, he refused. He went away very sorrowful; for he had great possessions. Ironically the great wealth that had made it easy for him to enter into life barred the entrance to eternal life.

This is what we mean by crisis in morality, by seeing the moral obligation in depth. The deeper a choice penetrates to the heart of experience, the more morally involved it becomes. Obeying the rule, even about killing, stealing, adultery, false witness and so on, is morally blunted if it does not call for struggle. This is what some have meant in their protests against what they call the moralizing tendency of modern life. We incline, they say, to see everything morally, which means setting things in good and bad categories when life situations are always too complex to yield to such simple treatment.

This is a relevant emphasis and yet it must not be allowed to deflect us from the stark fact that while rule-keeping is often a bloodless sort of moralism, beneath it lies the deep substratum of morality on which all vital, critical choosing must ultimately rest. It is dramatically set forth by Jesus' emphasis; in the first comment he referred to entering into life; in the second to being perfect. To enter life by being good may be a superficial understanding of moral obligation; but to want to be perfect lets the soul down into the depths of the moral struggle where one knows nothing of respite or self-approval.

The man went away sorrowful. How quickly his mood

seems to have changed from gaiety to depression. An odd reaction, we may think, for one who had great wealth. Little wonder that the disciples, for the most part poor, good men, were astonished. Bedazzled, perhaps, by the opulent stranger, they were dismayed that he was such a problem to himself.

Lao Tze is credited with having said: "Let nothing desirable be visible: this will save the people's minds from moral confusion." It may be said that the source of the rich young ruler's moral confusion was that the nature of the moral struggle was visible to him only on the level of rule and rubric. Had he been able to see the thing desirable—a righteousness based on the victories one wins beneath the surface—he might not have gone away sorrowful.

Would we?

10 THE CRISIS OF PIETY

> Not every one who says to me, "Lord, Lord" shall enter the kingdom of heaven, but he who does the will of my Father who is in heaven. On that day many will say to me, "Lord, Lord, did we not prophesy in your name, and cast out demons in your name, and do many mighty works in your name?" And then will I declare to them, "I never knew you; depart from me, you evildoers."
> MATTHEW 7:21-23

This is the saying of Jesus that separates the saint from the charlatan. It is either one of the most searching things he ever said or one of the most irresponsible—to the point almost of flippancy.

In times when loyalty to an individual teacher—of whom there must have been many—was the mark of serious religious devotion it was important that teacher and follower should know each other. Lack of formal academic credentials made this necessary; lack of organized schools—as we know them—made the name of the teacher serve both as identification and as talisman to the pupil. The Fourth Gospel, transferring the figure from school to flock, from teacher to shepherd, reports Jesus as saying: "The sheep hear his voice, and he calls his own sheep by name and leads them out. . . . I am the good shepherd; I know my own and my own know me" (John 10:3, 14). We would expect, therefore, to find this idea of mutual recognition, of the reciprocal relation between leader and friend, to appear during the latter days of Jesus' ministry. This is the case;

shortly before the feast of Unleavened Bread occurs the story of the inquirer who was concerned with the statistics of the saved. Jesus' reply took the form of a warning that parallels almost exactly the passage we are considering. He said there would be many at the last who would present their credits in terms of deeds done in his name. To which the bitter comment was to be made that he not only did not know them; he had no idea where they were from (Luke 13:23f).

However discomfiting this must have been, it was necessary that it be said. The external practices of piety come easy to most of those who indulge them. It is a simple matter to say "Lord, Lord." Saint and charlatan both speak it effortlessly. What it means to each is, however, a matter of vast difference. The surprise and shock the charlatan feels when he is told he is unrecognized is not the reaction of the saint, who, with the perversity that annoys us who are unsaintly, says he is not surprised, since his works were little worthy of regard and his name hardly worth remembering.

(1)

The difference between piety and its cheap counterfeit is discovered only when one looks beneath the surface of action to motive. And as Jesus, setting moral behavior within the dimension of depth, probed to the level of motive, he exposed a principle of immense gravity which says: it is good to do good, but good done from wrong motives is evil. Most of us are not prepared to go so far. We agree that good animated by unworthy or evil motives is a sort of second-rate goodness. We do not think, however, that it is bad. And yet if we look closely at what Jesus is saying we see emerging the shape of the problem of ends and means. We agree, in principle, that an evil means for a good end is morally disrespectable. Do we agree that a bad motive disqualifies a good deed? Let us not forget that the romantic figure of the devil represents him as a do-gooder, a dandy in topper and Inverness cape, open-handed and genial.

What was the motive here? The language of scripture suggests a kingdom and a password, or perhaps a key; two keys, indeed. Charlatan and saint are both concerned to get into the kingdom of heaven; each says "Lord, Lord," but only the one who does the will of the Father is allowed entrance. The "Lord" key does not work for everyone; the "will" key swings the portal open.

We are not surprised at this; it is simple common sense. The charlatan, however, does not like it. Suspicious "on that day" that his key will not work he comes up with a list of credits that, by any standard, are impressive. He prophesied in the Lord's name; he cast out demons, and did many mighty works. Perhaps our inclination is to disqualify the man by observing that there always have been false prophets who disguised their dishonesty by the sheep's clothing of piety; that being something of a devil himself, collusion with demons for some ultimate evil was not impossible for him; and of course "mighty works" sounds like boasting. The more meager one's efforts the greater likelihood of pretentious claims for their importance. Furthermore, mighty works can just as well be mighty in terms of evil as of good. History is filled with villainies that have been committed in the name of God.

This, we say, is simple common sense. Given time we can spot the hypocrite. Give him time and he will expose himself. But are we right in thinking that he is a conscious and calculating fraud? Jesus, who had his way with impostors does not judge them on this basis. He even goes so far as to disclaim any knowledge of them—"I never knew you." How then could he pass judgment on them. And yet he immediately turns and calls them evildoers; he *does* pass judgment on them and orders them out of his sight. What are we to make of this?

(2)

It was obviously something about which our Lord felt very deeply. In the other situation cited above we hear him saying to the shut-outs that despite their having eaten and drunk in his presence, thus breaking a social taboo against eating with dubious characters, and despite their having granted him freedom of speech for teaching ideas that were odious to them, he branded them as workers of iniquity and told them to go away. By what strange understanding of the values of tolerance could those who practiced them be called workers of iniquity? Is tolerance iniquitous? Are we not to be judged good or bad by what we do? If not, then pray by what are we to be judged? No wonder the victims of so sharp a judgment wept and gnashed their teeth. Who wouldn't?

We are confronted here by a penetration to levels of moral depth that lie far beneath our conventional observance of rules or the doing of good deeds. What is a good deed? Does it have the quality of goodness irrespective of the moral quality of the doer? Jesus once said that a good tree brings forth good fruit and an evil tree evil fruit. This is not the judgment of horticulture but of ethics, and it appears to mean that there is no truly good deed apart from a truly good doer. This distinguishes Jesus' idea of goodness from that of the existentialist who holds that the quality of a single action can be abstracted from the actor's total experience. Intention, design, aim, end, these all influence the doing of the act, but once it is done it stands in moral isolation from the doer.

In the view of Jesus there is no moral discontinuity between doer and deed however appearances on the surface may suggest it. It is not possible for a "worker of iniquity," to use Jesus' words, to do mighty works in his name. Whatever he does is evil. Though he cast out demons, or prophesy, he is still an "evil-doer."

This is strong medicine; we are far from willing to dose ourselves with it. For this reason we encounter moral charlatans as Jesus did. It is far easier to *do* good than to *be* good; hence the effort we make to appear good by doing good deeds. Is this not what Isaiah said: "Because this people draw near with their mouth and honor me with their lips, while their hearts are far from me, and their fear of me is a commandment of men learned by rote; therefore . . . the wisdom of their wise men shall perish, and the discernment of their discerning men shall be hid" (Isa. 29:13-14)?

It would seem to follow, therefore, that in the ethical consciousness of Jesus what the good man did was good, what the evil man did was evil. This takes us down to the moral continuum within which every separate act is set, or to the moral stratum where the essential difference between charlatan and saint is determined. As it is impossible to separate the moral quality of means and end so it is impossible to separate the moral quality of doer and deed. The evildoer, no matter how he cries "Lord, Lord," does not enter the kingdom of heaven; he who does the will of the "Father who is in heaven" shall enter, whether or not he speaks the exalted name.

(3)

If the charlatan is the man who, for his own selfish reasons, does good deeds in order to enter the kingdom of heaven and seeks to disguise his selfishness by saying "Lord, Lord," what is the saint? It is easy to spot the religious fraud even when he seeks, as the fraud will—consciously or unconsciously—to impress us with his piety; but the saint is not only in short supply, he is likely—consciously or unconsciously—to avoid the appearance of saintliness. Not because saintliness is distasteful to him but because he knows that its display is distasteful to others.

Nevertheless, Jesus' clear word is provided: "He who does the will of my Father." It is inescapable that the Father's will should be reduced to general rules for the guidance of those who want to do it. It is equally true that the Father's will cannot be embodied in a corpus of law. The legalist's problem lies in his never-finished effort to make new rules for new misdemeanors. Time may not make ancient good uncouth but it makes modern evil unpleasant. We shall always have the legalist with us and be grateful for him, but we must not forget that his efforts to make laws and our efforts to keep them will not create the kingdom of heaven.

The characteristic of the saint is not that he is lawless or willful but that he conforms to a deeper law and a higher will. Out of rules come the situations of behavior; out of the heart are the issues of life, and the heart of the saint beats with the rhythm of the Father's heart. When, therefore, he says "Lord, Lord," as he often will, it will not be to call attention to himself or to the "mighty works" he is doing; it will be the address of a jubilant and beholding soul to that which is the center of his being. When he is finally confronted with the fact that often when he gave his shirt to a naked beggar, a crust to a famished man, a word of encouragement to a prisoner, he was, in those "works," ministering to his great Friend, he will shrug it off with gentle embarrassment and say that he didn't remember it at all.

It is this sort of understanding of morality that sets piety in crisis. The Jews were a morally sensitive people and like all such they endangered true righteousness by the amplification of the Law. Always there were those within that God-oriented culture who cried out against the rituals that were the easy substitute for godliness. God, they said, cared nothing for the blood of sacrificed beasts, for rivers of votive oil. Yet it remained for Jesus to speak the most searching word: God was not only displeased; such "good works" were positive evil and those who performed them were not simply recognized as workers of iniquity, they were not even noticed at all. The stoic will be able, perhaps, to stand up under the rebuke of God but what can endure His rejection?

In an angry passage in *The Communist Manifesto,* Karl Marx said: "Law, morality, and religion are to the proletarian so many bourgeois prejudices behind which lurk just as many bourgeois interests." We do not like that sort of talk. Do we like any better what Jesus said, when it is set in a pattern similar to what we have quoted: "Prophesy, casting out demons, and doing mighty works are to the charlatan so many Christian practices behind which lurk just as many evil interests?" Not very much better!

11 THE CRISIS OF SUCCESS

"Command that these two sons of mine may sit, one at your right hand and one at your left, in your kingdom." But Jesus answered, "You do not know what you are asking. Are you able to drink the cup that I am to drink?" MATTHEW 20:21-22

We ought to be able to say without protective argument that what we all want is security and success. These twin ambitions are so much alike that they are often thought identical: to be successful is to be secure; to be secure is to be successful. This is not only the case with those whose measure of both is the stockmarket or one's monthly bank statement. It is similarly true for artist and theologian, statesman and scientist.

Success and insecurity would also seem to be the same in their inaccessibility. In another connection, the point has been that security is impossible, that one's sense of security is inverse to the aggregate of the things thought to guarantee it. The more things one acquires to protect him the more vulnerable he is to loss or pillage. Man's only security is insecurity. The same is true of success: the higher the index of success the less satisfied one is likely to feel. The most famous success in literature is a man who had to build new barns to store his glut of grain, and the verdict he won was that he was a fool.

Of course this sounds perverse to a success-security culture like our own. So we shrug off Professor Hocking's observation that "no religion is a true religion which does not make men tingle to their fingertips with a sense of infinite hazard." Or when the late G. K. Chesterton said, "Nothing succeeds like failure," we say he was simply having fun with words.

Now this is not a morbid judgment on the result of man's struggles, the formulation of a fate that reduces to ultimate futility his dreams, his wisdom and his dexterity. To abandon success and security is to renege on life; he who seeks failure must follow it to death. What we are saying is that these natural goals of the human spirit are to be sought and found, if found at all, on levels much deeper than the bright surfaces where their glare so easily dazzles and blinds us. And it is exactly this fact that explains the episode of the mother of the sons of Zebedee and her maternal concern that they be made both successful and secure, one on the right, the other on the left in the promised kingdom.

(1)

We must be careful not to judge this woman unkindly. She is identified by some as Salome, who with Mary Magdalene stood by the mother of Jesus during the anguish of the crucifixion and who later visited the tomb with unguents for the lifeless body. If this surmise is correct it should indicate that the confidence with which she had approached the mighty friend of her undistinguished sons was not diminished by what seems, to a careless reading, a summary dismissal of her hopes.

It is natural for mothers to want their sons to succeed. This may make them overprotective and thus result in an impairment of their sense of self-reliance. Such success as James and John had won as fishermen was, we judge, less than spectacular. All we know of them is the nickname the violence of their tempers had won them: Sons of Thunder. It is easy for us to dabble with psychoanalysis at this impossible distance, and infer that their vehemence may have been overcompensation for a deeply concealed sense of failure.

We do not need this sophisticated inference, however, to account for the solicitude of their mother. The amazing Galilean who had invited her sons to join him in the establishment of the kingdom of heaven seemed able to do anything. If he was serious about this kingdom business he would have to give it some organizational structure. And that involved a man, right and left, as the next in command to himself. With the proper confidence that her two boys—now suddenly in her fond eyes grown to potential rulers in a kingdom—were the men for the key posts, Salome made the request.

Her suggestion was as bold as the opportunity was unique. When had fishermen ever been elevated to the seats of the mighty? Perhaps she remembered stories about a shepherd, the son of Jesse, who became the greatest of Israel's kings. Was it beyond the sons of Zebedee to rule if given the appointment? And yet part of the difficulty lay just there: she thought of the possibility of success by appointment. Give a man a big job and he will become a big man. This is one of the half-truths of our success culture. How easy it would be to escape the mediocrity that too often plagues us if it were true. Unhappily it is quite as often the case that a big job exposes all the littleness that may be in the man who is appointed to it.

Jesus did not comment academically on the nature of success. Instead he put his finger on the point the mother overlooked. Such appointments are not to be had by command; they are reserved for those for whom they are prepared by the Father. This may have puzzled her since there was no way for taking her request to the higher authority. What was clear, however, was that she did not know what she was asking for. It was not, as she thought, distinction, power, responsibility; it was a cup of bitterness. And when, turning from the mother's importunity to the sober sons who stood by, Jesus asked whether they could drink the cup he was to drink, they soberly replied: "We are able."

This was a strange way for one to speak who spoke of himself as the pretender to a throne. Was he unimpressed with the glamour of a throne? Did he see dominion only as the drinking of a bitter cup? To be a king is to know the rancor of rule, but how many kings had spoken of the royal role as a cup of gall? Surely the immense satisfactions of dominion over multitudes could sweeten any cup and provide to the whole line of the kings' favorite appointees delights sufficient to overbalance their trials.

(2)

The indignation of the ten, upon overhearing the mother's request, is understandable. It was not due to any loftier ideas that they had about success. More likely it was their sudden realization that they had been outmaneuvered, and by the mother of two men who, if they wanted advantage, might have, at least, pressed for it themselves. The other men did not have their mothers along to ask for favors.

Jesus called them together. We wonder if Salome was within earshot when he gave them his famous formula for success. He was too wise to reproach them for their wish to achieve position and authority. Man is so endowed that not to succeed is to fail and not to want to succeed is worse: surrender. Indeed Jesus himself wanted to succeed; to succeed so completely that he turned his back resolutely on all the cheap and easy tricks by which success was promised him in the forty wilderness days after his appointment to success at his baptism. To have scoffed at achievement would not only have falsified human nature; it would have aspersed the purposes of God withal.

But there are two ways of achieving it. The whole memorable proposition needs to be spelled out:

> You know that the rulers of the Gentiles lord it over them, and their great men exercise authority over them. It shall not be so among you; but whoever would be great among you must be your servant, and whoever would be first among you must be your slave; even as the Son of man came not to be served but to serve, and to give his life as a ransom for many. [Matt. 20:25-28]

The way of the Gentiles, and the way of the Son of Man; these were the options before the twelve after the proposal of Salome had been disallowed.

The "rulers of the Gentiles" were successful men as were also "their great men." How they achieved lordship, greatness and authority makes little difference. It could have been by diligence, shrewdness, heredity, appointment or deceit. The point, however, is the manner in which they used what success had put into their hands. A Greek preposition (kata) gives them away. This little word means "down from" or "down upon" and thus conveys an emphasis not felt in our word "over." What Jesus said was that the rulers of the Gentiles lorded it *down;* the great men exercised authority *down.* Two things followed: first, the continued success of the rulers and the great depended on their keeping on top of others. This equated success with superior position and that meant they were successful only as long as their subjects were unsuccessful, and from that came oppression and tyranny. The second result was the corruption of those whose success had made them powerful. Jesus described this as the way of the Gentiles and said it was not to be so with his friends. Did he see how easy it would be for the thunderous sons of Zebedee to fall into this pattern and be victimized by it?

Jesus' idea of success and its uses turns the Gentile idea upside down. Rule, greatness and the exercise of authority were to be abjured for the status of servant and slave. Greatness to the servant, priority to the slave. Instead of exercising one's powers from above downward, one was to exercise one's powers from below upward. This also had two results: first, the success of the slave was estimated in terms of the service he could give to others; and second, the servant, sincerely ministering to others, was measurably spared the corruptions of high position and power.

(3)

It needs to be said that the charlatan will shrewdly see that he can appropriate the role of the servant and even the manners of the slave in order that he may win his way to the top. And once at the top he will become the most cruel of oppressors. Was it because Jesus saw this possibility that he followed his formula for success with the words "even as" and adduced the Son of Man as its exemplar? Surely the giving of one's life in ransom for many is at the opposite pole from the oppressive power of the great in the exploitation of many. This is again the difference between the charlatan and the saint; the last thing the impostor will give away is his life.

And it needs also to be asked whether the pattern Jesus proposed for his friends was followed by himself. Yet to ask it is to answer it. What sort of a success was he? It seems almost impious to raise the question. Even those modern rulers of the Gentiles who count success in opposite terms concede, not only that he was a success but that in a strange way he has made countless others successful to the extent to which they have been willing to make service the meaning of achievement.

This, we confess, sets success within a dimension that is too deep for us. Nevertheless when we encounter, in the midst of a culture that sees success in the shallows, those who discover the deeps within which it must lie, we respond with a wistful sort of gratitude.

What of Albert Schweitzer as a success? Is there any gauge by which his ransoming life can be measured? What made William Faulkner say recently that success—the Gentile kind—has become so easy that we have lost the capacity to be humble (servant and slave)? And how often has the famous letter of William James to Mrs. Henry Whitman (June 7, 1899) been quoted? In its closing lines, he described the frenzied pursuit of success as "ebullitions of spleen, quite unintelligible to anyone but myself." The fact is there are many besides him to whom what he wrote is altogther intelligible. We understand him with frightening clarity. Listen:

> I am against all big successes and big results; and in favor of the eternal forces of truth which always work in the individual and immediately unsuccessful way [servant of all?], underdogs always [slaves?], till history comes and puts them on the top.

How successful is Jesus' kind of success? Does it avoid the vulgarization Professor James despised? Are its accumulations ever lost? Are the opportunities for its expansion ever limited? Is the warmth of its inner satisfactions ever cooled?

What answer would the mother of the sons of Zebedee give these questions now? Perhaps she answered them then. At least it is reassuring that when we last see her she is standing near a cross, whereon was dying the incarnate success of God.

12 THE CRISIS OF DEDICATION

And they were on the road, going up to Jerusalem, and Jesus was walking ahead of them; and they were amazed, and those who followed were afraid. And taking the twelve again, he began to tell them what was to happen to him, saying, "Behold, we are going up to Jerusalem; and the Son of man will be delivered to the chief priest and the scribes, and they will condemn him to death, and deliver him to the Gentiles; and they will mock him, and spit upon him, and scourge him, and kill him; and after three days he will rise. MARK 10:32-34

In another connection we have already considered security and success and the problems they present to those who understand them deeply. With what appears to be a strange sort of perversity they seem to be both goals for human striving and penalties for human achievement. Tillich [1] notes that "there may be something in the structure of our institutions which produces illness in more and more people. It may, for instance, be that the unlimited, ruthless competition which deprives everybody of a feeling of security, makes many in our healthy nation sick; not only those who are unsuccessful in competition, but also those who are most successful." The result of this is a subconscious desire for sickness as an escape from the rigors of the demand for security in an insecure world. And this partially explains the widely observed increase of mental illness and instability.

[1] Paul Tillich, *The New Being*, Scribner's, 1955, pp. 35 f.

Confronted by a not dissimilar condition in his own time, our Lord undertook to help his friends understand success and security within the dimensions of depth. What he said is apparently as unpalatable to our times as it was to his own. How ready are we to understand insecurity as security; failure as success; self-denial as the essence of self-affirmation?

(1)

There is another experience common to all the sons of men which befell Jesus a very few days before his death. It had to do with the measure of his dedication to what he believed was his appointed—and accepted—role. We waive, for the moment, the question as to whether he was more deeply aware of his destiny than we can be of our own. It is enough to note the fact that far too often, when our dedication is under test, we find it convenient to shift our loyalty to something less difficult.

We cannot live without loyalties; we must be dedicated or die. This necessity has its origin in the native sense of dependence with which we are born. The ultimate attachment we feel for a great cause is simply the conscious and deliberate enlargement of the instinctive hunger that draws the infant to its mother's breast. Since, as we grow older, our choices tend to become less instinctual and more deliberate, they are more and more affected by circumstances we cannot control. Hence our shifting loyalties, our wavering dedications.

That Jesus' loyalty was deep, fixed and irrevocable stands in stark contrast to the vacillations of his inner circle at the time when the dedication of both was torn by growing tensions. The story we have before us presents dedication in crisis in dramatic form.

In a fashion not easy for us to understand, Jerusalem was a symbolic focus of loyalty felt by every faithful son of Israel. Its history was magnetic: the holy city, the holy Temple, the holy ritual. In Jesus' day the new temple, built by Herod the Great, was a shining monument of white marble and gold. "Thither the tribes go up," said its poets, drawn by an impulse of loyalty we rarely feel toward cities. It was the focus of recollection, of power and of pious practices. The tombs of the prophets were there, venerated by those who kept white their sepulchers to preserve their memory. Once a year, or oftener if convenient, the faithful Jew visited the city. It was perhaps as much an act of defiance of Rome as of dedication to Israel.

As a loyal son, Jesus was sensitive to this impulse, but the pilgrimage which with strange prescience he knew to be his last was, we assume, less easily undertaken than earlier visits had been. It was no perfunctory holiday jaunt; it was something against which we saw immense barriers heaving themselves in his track, from which less dauntless dedication would have turned back without shame or self-pity. Something in the way he walked seems to have impressed the man who later was going to record the episode. Luke says "he set his face" (R. S. V.) and earlier versions put it "steadfastly." The necessity that compelled him communicated itself to face and pace.

The twelve, who in all likelihood took their journey in a more casual fashion, "were amazed." He had a way of surprising them, and yet they apparently never quite got used to it. "Those who followed," meaning, we assume, the miscellaneous fellow wayfarers, "were afraid." It is not easy for us to grasp the meaning of this reaction. They did not fear him and what lay before him; even if they had foreseen it, they were most likely to escape. The least we can make of this is that the intensity of the mood of Jesus, as he "was walking ahead of them," was so acute as to be manifest to all who saw him. Both of the words that describe the crowd reaction are powerful: amazement, astonishment, awe; fear, terror, portent. Little wonder that they felt something unusual was ahead.

(2)

But what was ahead? In the holiday mood it was to be expected that the festival experiences awaited them. And though in troubled times such as those in which they were living almost anything might happen, the twelve and the crowd were not looking for trouble. We may even assume that had trouble been foreseen they would, without compunction, have turned back. The feast days came and went and there was no point in going up to Jerusalem just to invite trouble. Insurrections behaved that way, not pilgrimages.

So Jesus told them what was awaiting him beyond the Mount of Olivet. Why? Because, perhaps, while amazement may attract, it also has within it the important element of uncertainty that restrains; and while fear may drive some to the fanatical boldness of desperation, it is for most the signal for retreat to a safer salient. Their amazement and fear had to be given reasons, reasons, paradoxically, that gave determination to his face and steadiness to his footsteps. He did not attempt to soften the realities. His dedication was in process of its sorest testing since, perhaps, the forty wilderness days, but it was not to be supported by evasion or illusion. He was soon to encounter and be delivered over to those who had, up to this time, unsuccessfully tried to lay hold on him; at their hands he would be condemned to death for nothing he had done and be put to death by Gentiles who cared very little about what he had done. And he would be a likely victim for the brutal sport they made of prisoners and before they killed him he was to hear their vulgar mockery and insult and feel their torture.

"And after three days he will rise."

It is not easy to think of a schedule of possible horrors more complete or more calculated to bleach one's face of color and drain one's legs of strength, or to give one better reason for turning back. This is what he saw; this is what he told his friends they would see though they were not certainly to be implicated in the peril. Had he already foreseen that in the prospect of danger defection would scatter them to places of safety? Perhaps; and the likelihood of their desertion was, in its way, the hardest thing he was to face.

Somehow the judgment of men has never convicted Jesus of bravado in this instance or accused him of willfully courting destruction. Nor is this merely the wish to be kind to the memory of one who otherwise deserves the greatest honor. On the contrary, if we see this experience within the proper dimensions, it exposes the true meaning of dedication in crisis. His loyalty was so fixed and sure that it could not be unsteadied by any possible combination of spiritual and physical tortures that threatened it. We wonder what happened to the amazement and fear of those to whom he spelled out the portending terror. There is little in the record that tells us. Elsewhere we are told they understood nothing; not until after his death did they remember and reconstruct his predictions. Was it simple dullness of heart or a stolid sort of attachment insensitive to deep feelings? As Mark continues the story, James and John put forth their claim to special privilege but not, as we discover, with any idea that they were likely to run into difficulty.

(3)

We must not overlook his confidence in ultimate triumph. That the Son of Man would, after three days, rise again had specific reference to Jesus' own experience; it also has general reference to the faith that activates all deep dedication. This faith is what denies the tragic facts of life the right to determine the meaning of life. To quote Tillich again: [2] "It is the courage

[2] *Ibid.,* p. 53.

to say yes to one's own life and life in general, in spite of the driving forces of fate, in spite of the insecurities of daily existence, in spite of the catastrophes of existence and the breakdown of meaning."

It is idle to speculate what might have happened if Jesus, anticipating what lay immediately ahead of him, had changed his plans in the interests of security. It is equally idle to speculate as to whether such a possibility was not open to him. Of course it was, and the cup he saw offered him in the shadows of Gethsemane is proof of that. To understand what would have happened had his dedication faltered we need only to look at his friends whose dedication, however boldly confessed, was "bound in shallows and in miseries." Panic, flight, violence, denial—the record is not a pretty one.

And yet, who are we to find fault? It is not reassuring to discover how thin is the topsoil of loyalty that covers the subsoil of our distrust. Not long ago the Chief Justice of the United States Supreme Court said he doubted that the Bill of Rights, if submitted to the American people in a referendum, would today be approved. Is this reluctance because within the past ten years many who have stood up to attest their dedication to the rights by which a free society exists, have been, in words mordantly familiar, "delivered to the chief priests and scribes" to be mocked and scourged?

We have been told, no doubt to the point of irritation, that it is the dedication of the hard core of disciplined Communists who fear not priest and scribe, nor mockery and death, who infuse a world conspiracy with vital power.

How deep is our loyalty to sobriety, to essential and impartial justice to all, to the priority of law over power, to the necessity of moral integrity between means and ends, to the inherent God-spark in every man despite his colossal follies and his corrupting sins, to the invincibility of love in a hate-frightened world, to the kingdom of heaven *now?*

Loyal? Of course. Dedicated? By all means; for these are the elements of which our culture is compounded. To disavow them is to turn our faces away from Jerusalem, that imperishable symbol of political and religious power and idealism. Betrayal, however, comes not alone by disavowal; it comes also by the diminished faith that stops short of the city's gates.

It is not difficult to gauge the depth of our dedication. If, when we see some utterly dedicated soul "walking ahead of us," we are first amazed that such devotion is possible, and then afraid because of what may happen to him—and because of him to us—our loyalty is shallow. And shallowness makes for faintness of heart, and it is the fainthearted who, instead of kneeling in triumph in Gethsemane, rise to flee in panic into its heavy darkness.

"He who has ears to hear, let him hear."

13 THE CRISIS OF CONFLICT

I came to cast fire on the earth; and would that it were already kindled! I have a baptism to be baptized with; and how I am constrained until it is accomplished! Do you think that I have come to give peace on earth? No, I tell you, but rather division; for henceforth in one house there will be five divided, three against two and two against three; they will be divided, father against son and son against father, mother against daughter and daughter against her mother, mother-in-law against her daughter-in-law and daughter-in-law against her mother-in-law. LUKE 12:49-53

How nice it would be if life were uncomplicated and serene. This latent wish is partly the reason why the demagogue who interprets life in simple terms and promises easy solutions gets a following. Also, the fact that life is not simple and easy explains why, sooner or later, his followers leave him.

We cannot remind ourselves too often of the necessity for using metaphor, even in describing the most elemental affairs. The more complex a situation the greater likelihood that we shall describe it pictorially. Thus, in the words that engage our interest here, we instinctively react to Jesus' inflammatory language as we do to metaphor. He really did not mean, we say, to cast fire on the earth; this was simply his way of dramatizing a trying situation. Can we picture him as fomenting strife and division and tugging at the leash of restraint until he could do it? Arsonist, pyromaniac, vandal, destroyer—these are the last words we would even think of applying to him. If he ever conceived of his vocation in such terms, the ages have thoroughly misunderstood him. Was this the gentle figure who said "peace I leave with you" to a group of frightened friends? How can the Prince of Peace be the destroyer of families? If we are to have any understanding of this distressful passage it is to be found on levels far beneath the surface of life's simplicities.

(1)

One wonders what recollections prompted his use of the firebrand metaphor. The ancient story of Sodom and Gomorrah consumed by the hot anger of Jehovah? The city of Jerusalem had repeatedly been burned and looted and was shortly to be left in ruins again, not by His kindling torch but at the hands of Vespasian. Had Jesus ever heard of the awesome holocaust of mighty Carthage, less than two thousand miles from where he stood and two hundred years away? "The whole city was burnt, the ruins were plowed to express final destruction, and a curse was invoked with great solemnities upon anyone who might attempt to rebuild it." [1] Rome had a macabre delight in pointing to that job when her subject peoples stirred rebelliously. Even today we use the phrase "Carthaginian peace" with a shudder of horror.

Not only fire; baptism. This was surely no deeply satisfying acceptance of appointment, laved in the tepid water of the Jordan, brightened by the hovering wings of a dove and accredited by a proud, approving voice from heaven. It was rather an initiation into the cult of the disturbers of the earth, a bitter and bloody bath, suggested perhaps by the taurobolium of the Mithraists.

[1] H. G. Wells, *Outline of History*, Macmillan, 1920, Vol. II, p. 485.

Not only fire and blood to which he was committed, but earth? No, I tell you, but rather division." Even that sanctuary of security, the home, was to be riven by hostilities that would not be easily composed since the ratio between the embattled was to be always close: three to two, and two to three. The folly of trusting one's dearest was to be manifested by the discovery that one's enemies were of one's own household.

What are we to make of this? Is it enough to point out that the pressures under which he was being slowly crushed were so great as to change radically his earlier understandings of his mission and message? This external factor cannot be discounted, but we cannot believe that it made him equivocate or doubt; that he found himself torn between the opposites of peace and conflict, or that, for the moment, he had abandoned one role to accept its opposite. The swing of the mood pendulum between exaltation and despair may have been a real part of his experience as the Son of Man, and yet, somehow we are unsatisfied with emotional schizophrenia as the explanation of such contrary words as, for example, "Whatever house you enter, first say, 'Peace be to this house!' "; and, "I have come to set a man against his father. . . . and a man's foes will be those of his own household."

What is clearly seen here to be conflict is also to be seen as critical because it represented to him an understanding of the human situation within the dimension of depth. Only within recent years has it become generally accepted that the psyche responds to life by what is known as ambivalence, defined simply as "simultaneous conflicting feelings toward a person or thing, as love and hate." [2] When this knowledge is able to direct our thinking about ourselves and our circumstances we are

[2] *Webster's New World Dictionary of the American Language,* World Publishing Co., 1954.

measurably spared the dangerous feelings of pride on the one hand, or guilt on the other, which accompany or follow our opposite moods.

(2)

Superficially life takes on the aspect of either-or. A man is good or bad, shrewd or stupid, gentle or violent, chaste or lascivious, happy or morose. Therefore in any given situation we will be able to predict how the good man and the bad man will act. If the behavior of either deviates from his recognized pattern we are puzzled, or pained, or scandalized. Some extraordinary overpowering compulsion is assigned the role of *agent provocateur*, or maybe temporary insanity will do for an explanation. Since every mood is autonomous as long as it lasts we make the mistaken inference that the spirit is univalent. Thus ambivalence appears to us as split personality and indecision is the sign of weakness instead of vitality.

Now it should appear to be important that the critical conflict which characterized the last days of our Lord's earthly life lends itself to a much more profound interpretation than we have often assigned to it. Life, deeply seen, is not bothered so much by the illusions of peace or strife, security or calamity, success or failure, standing in radical isolation from each other; it is represented as a dialectic movement between extremes, or paradoxically, as a compound of what appear to be opposites.

Jesus stood up to the awesome fact that he who brings peace casts fire on the earth; he who brings unity causes division, he who loves his family hates it. This is not double-talk. He lives in cloud Cuckoo-land who expects planetary peace without the birth pains through which peace is born. Within the dimensions of the world's life today, unity comes first by the voluntary separations that alone save unity from being coerced. Where else than in the circle of the family is there greater devotion and more fierce competitiveness? With those we love best the sense of estrangement can cut deepest. We are unconcerned about those we do not know, mildly concerned with those we know slightly; deeply concerned with those we know well, radically involved with those whose lives are a part of our own. It is out of the deep well of intimacy that the sweet water of love and the bitter waters of hate are drawn. Does not this cast a beam of light on a much vexed verse that has Jesus saying that unless we hate our parents and possessions the kingdom of heaven is not for us?[3] The kingdom is not made up of haters; it is crowded with ambivalent souls! The woman who was a great sinner was forgiven much. To the easily tempted this means: let sin abound that grace may more richly abound. The more searching mind of Paul saw its deeper meaning. Why, in all conscience, should we rejoice as Jesus admonished, when men despitefully use us? Because only those capable of accepting despite are capable also of giving devotion. The way in which this clarifies the psychological subtleties of the masculine and feminine components in both sexes and complicates the growing problem of homosexuality in our times[4] is out of bounds to this discussion except as it parallels the principal thesis.

Jesus, we are saying, refused to take flight from the realities of human experience by looking for the peace of mind that comes—if indeed it comes at all—by vacuity of mind. He might have banished the negative thought of a destroying fire by

[3] Luke 14:26. Cf. also II Cor. 6:8-10: "In honor and dishonor, in ill repute . . . impostors, and yet . . . true; unknown, and yet well known; as dying, and behold we live; as punished and yet not killed; as sorrowful, yet always rejoicing; as poor, yet making many rich; as having nothing, and yet possessing everything."

[4] Cf. Abram Kardiner, *The Flight from Masculinity: Sex and Morality*, Bobbs-Merrill, 1954, pp. 160 f.

thinking only of green pastures and still waters. Why dignify one's daily baptism of pain—how glibly we speak of our various baptisms: fire, blood, et cetera—by giving it a thought; think rather of the sweet euphoria of the springtime. Why look with morbid concentration at the divisions that separate men when— again how glibly we say it—there is more that unites us than divides?

The reason for refusing such folly is that it is a denial both of the nature of life and of the human spirit; of life because it is simply not true that it comes to us in mutually exclusive categories; of the mind because its fallibility makes it incapable of sharpening issues into mutually exclusive categories. To say this does not solve one problem without raising others. Nor is it an invitation to despair or a justification of moral flaccidity. It merely states the proposition that within community there is division, within peace there is conflict, within security there is insecurity, within success there is failure, within love there is hate. We are never asked to shut our eyes to dichotomy within unity; we are asked only to see life within a dimension spacious enough to accommodate the consuming fire and the benediction of peace, the judgment of God and His forgiving mercy.

And if, oppressed by this ambivalence, we yearn for simplicities we cannot have, or accept the inanities peddled by charlatans, let us recall that Jesus, confronted by the same paradox, said: "How I am constrained until it is accomplished" (Luke 12:50).

(3)

This self-exposure of Jesus points up an ancient—and current—misemphasis of the Christian witness to the effect that to be a follower of Christ is to take leave of the contradictions and the defeats of life. One is exhorted simply to yield oneself up, to give oneself to Christ and thereby come instantaneously into undisturbed and undisturbable calm. But the Christian profession is no prophylaxis against pain, disappointment or even despair. To say that "Christ is the answer" is true only if we ask the right question. If we ask for the resolution of all conflict we must not be disillusioned if we hear him say: "In the world you will have tribulation." If, however, we ask for an explanation of life's irrationalities and contraries within a dimension of depth we may be prepared to hear him say: "But be of good cheer, I have overcome the world." The Greek word *kosmos* so easily recognized as "world" means, more precisely, the aggregate of sensitive existence!

The peace of the Christian is not the absence, the cessation or the adjournment of conflict. As Studdert-Kennedy put it familiarly:

> Peace does not mean the end of all our striving,
> Joy does not mean the drying of our tears;
> Peace is the power that comes to souls arriving
> Up to the light where God Himself appears.[5]

This understanding of peace, joy, power and light is why Christianity is not a religion of withdrawal or negation but of acceptance and affirmation. It is also why the amulet that promises to ward off evil or the scapular that offers the soldier at best a prompt escort to heaven and at least exemption from injury have no proper place in Christian usage.

This paradox is also why the Christian must see conflict in depth. Only thus is the ambivalence of Jesus made intelligible: lose life and save it, deny self and achieve selfhood, humble the self and be exalted. Thus also, we believe, is the conflict in the cosmos between good and evil or—if we prefer—between God

[5] "The Suffering God," from *The Sorrows of God* by G. A. Studdert-Kennedy, Harper, 1924. Used by permission of the publisher.

and all that stands in opposition to Him to be understood; and we must be brought to see the eternity of conflict, life dying and striving to be born, the enchantment of the hope of a heaven and the terror of a hell, all within the dimension of depth.

With simple fairness Jesus once said to those whose attachment to him had involved them in a dangerous enterprise: "A disciple is not above his teacher, nor a servant above his master" (Matt. 10:24). This followed explicit instructions that could hardly have reassured them: "You will be hated by all for my name's sake . . . When they persecute you in one town, flee to the next" (Matt. 10:22-23). Once they were committed, however, they were not free to opt the easy and refuse the difficult. No less difficult is it for us who profess discipleship, to see ourselves both as fire-casters and as peace-makers without falsifying our devotion.

We shall not resolve the paradox because life ultimately defies our resolving. But we can keep in our hearts and before our minds two facts: First, the deeper we go into the experience of living the less frightening does paradox become; and second, in the words of a familiar hymn:

> It is the way the Master trod
> Should not the servant tread it still.

14 THE CRISIS OF TRIUMPH

And they brought the colt to Jesus, and threw their garments
on it; and he sat upon it. And many spread their garments on the
road, and others spread leafy branches which they had cut from
the fields. And those who went before and those who followed
cried out, "Hosanna! Blessed be he who comes in the name of the
Lord! Blessed be the kingdom of our father David that is coming!
Hosanna in the highest!" And he entered Jerusalem, and went into
the temple; and when he had looked round at everything, as it
was already late, he went out to Bethany with the twelve. MARK
11:7-10

To strive for success, whether it be moral, social, material, intellectual—or even to strive for failure—is to respond to an inner
urgency toward fulfillment that we cannot resist. How carefully
we collect and save the bright little fragments of achievement
that, in their aggregate, represent to us the measure of success.
And when the sum of our salvage gives to us a moment of
respite and to our fellows an occasion for applause, we call
success by its more radiant name: Triumph. Triumph is to
success what victory is to conquest;[1] the moment when the
struggle is over, the final decision announced.

Conflict must have an issue: the fire to be cast on the earth
and the baptism to be undergone must be "accomplished" and
we have seen that it will not come about by the elimination of

[1] Rom. 8:37, R.S.V.: "We are *more* than conquerors."

one or the other of the contestants. This rigor is not easy for us to accept and so we are prey to palliatives that promise us the security and success which, within the total dimensions of life, are not to be had. Nor does this mean that we are fated to fail, doomed to insecurity. It means that all success, that every conquest carries its freight of failure and defeat even while it raises the standard under which it advances or falters.

(1)

It is interesting that the last entrance of Jesus into Jerusalem has so long been called triumphant. The word "entrance" has delightful connotations: as a noun, accented on the first syllable, it means primarily the place or the moment of entering; as a verb, accented on the last syllable, it means to delight, to enrapture, to charm. The words in their Latin origins fit more comfortably our mood for such an occasion; the Greek says, with stark simplicity, simply that Jesus went into the city. In the telling of an episode this difference though slight is important. When Jesus went into the city there was an entrance—on a beast accompanied by crowds—and he entranced the holiday-makers—they shouted the word of acclaim reserved only for kings.

Nevertheless, all of this appears far from the mind of Jesus. As he seems not to have been concerned with an entrance he was similarly unconcerned with an exit. We recall the words: "As it was already late, he went out to Bethany with the twelve."

Of course the word "triumph" does not occur in the record, but a careless look at what took place makes its use easy. Was there something in the minds of those who have left us the story that made them try to rescue one moment of brightness from the otherwise somber circumstances of the last week? We do not know; but what is fairly clear is that the aspect we call triumph seems not to have been planned by him. We must not regard the display that we make on Palm Sunday as a reproduction of what it is designed to remember. The road-weary Jesus wanted a beast to ride, not a parade. His request for a mount to carry him was, in retrospect, said to be a sign of his awareness of his royalty. But surely, astride the foal of an ass he was hardly more than a caricature of a king on a horse. Had he designed it thus, it must be thought a delightful bit of satire, acted instead of spoken.

It was not only out of character for him to affect or ape royalty entering the great gate; everything that happened fails to fit the picture of him we have seen up to this point. He was going to Jerusalem to worship, not to be crowned. The noisy acclaim, confused and disturbing, gathered about him by a strange caprice of the crowd. Had he been pleased by it, had he thought it an explosive demonstration of a success he had, for a time, feared he would not win, he might have been expected to rally the mob and to set up an organization for consolidating his triumph.

We may even properly re-examine what the crowd thought. They cried "Hosanna!" which means "save us." This was more a call for help than a shout of victory. The pilgrims were far from certain about the identity of the man who rode silent and unresponsive in the surging throng. He was son of David, a tattered title of honor; he was king—this was a grim irony; he was a prophet from Galilee. Well; there was realism in naming his home and his vocation; but Galilee was a place of ferment where revolts were quickly born and quickly suffocated; and prophets—who had ever heard of a prophet indulging the luxury of a mount to take him to town? As for the Pharisees who had seen millions come to feast days and return, this was no coronation parade; it was a traffic hazard and a general nuisance.

44266

(2)

Is there any clear indication of our Lord's reaction to the spectacle? As he went into the city there was apparently little evidence of enthusiasm on his part. Such as it was, in any case, was quickly spent and his mind was taken over by a more somber mood. His perfunctory look about the temple and retreat to Bethany, not with the acclaim of a crowd but with twelve silent, bewildered men, plodding behind him—this sight seems in a stroke to cancel even the recollection of the noisy hour so recently spent on the great road to the great gate.

All this may be seen as a continuation of the mood that shook him when the golden dome of the Temple first caught his eye as he rounded the shoulder of Olivet. Tears had blurred the sight; he had wept and cried aloud, not the words of triumph but of death. His own death—for he knew he was going to the city that killed the prophets of his people; the death also of the city that destroyed the spokesmen of God; the death also of a great dream. How often he would have taken the great city to his heart but it would not. Desolation was to be the reward of its defection from God. Did he suddenly change his mind, once the sight of the doomed city was momentarily hidden as they dipped down into valley of the Kidron before the final ascent? Hardly; indeed the awful fact was that the general blindness that could not see the hour of the city's visitation was dramatically exhibited by the miscellaneous jocularity of the carefree feastgoers who walked beside him.

Of course we have in mind the fact that the accounts of the reporters who covered the incident are varied. One says he cleansed the Temple, an act, it can be plausibly argued, of desperation. Many times before he had invaded its courts but never with anger and violence. And it was in the days immediately following that he made his most poignant comment about the relation of the use of the means of violence to achieve the ends of piety: "All who take the sword will perish by the sword" (Matt. 26:52). Another writer says that in the interval between coming into the city and withdrawing to Bethany he conducted a brief open-air clinic for the blind and the lame in the Temple area. Despite these disparities in details, the general impression produced by the various aspects of the story is uniform: whatever else the entrance into the city was, it was not a triumph.

If we want the true quality of his state of mind we must think of this experience not in terms of triumph but of victory. Two things point this up: just before the crowds moved into the last stretch of the road to the city, a blind beggar, the son of Timaeus, jostled by the heedless and rebuked by the heartless, had attracted the Galilean's attention. What was the meaning of holiday to him? Little, except perhaps a more generous take from the larger crowds. Jesus called him and asked what he wanted. "Let me receive my sight," he answered. "Go your way," Jesus said. "Your faith has made you well." In that miracle-moment one man's world was changed from darkness to light and "he followed him on the way." We do not forget the words put into Jesus' mouth by the fourth evangelist: "I am the light of the world; he who follows me will not walk in darkness, but will have the light of life" (John 8:12) This was victory; triumph was to be delayed until all eyes were opened.

The second pointer was his address to the disciples after the ill-considered request of the mother of Zebedee's sons. Great men among the Gentiles, he had said, exercise authority over them. They are the men on horseback, lifted above the heads of the masses, always looking and talking down to them. This was not his way, nor theirs. If he had ever, in imagination, cast himself in the role of king, in those words he completely repudiated the notion, both for himself and his followers. This was victory; triumph was to be delayed until all men saw that those who would be great must be servants and slaves.

(3)

As we have observed in other connections, this is not easy to take, and yet it is inescapable if we see triumph in crisis—if we see victory within the dimension of depth. We all are pleased by the acclaim of people; it is native to the soul and when it represents victory—however slight or brief—we call it triumph. Indeed we must think that our Lord also enjoyed it. The indignation of certain scribes at the applause of children in the Temple won deserved rebuke from the object of their childish delight. "Have you never read, 'Out of the mouths of babes and sucklings thou has brought perfect praise'?" (Matt. 21:16).

The difference, we believe, lies in our Lord's capacity for keeping a distinction between victory and triumph, between that measure of success that is possible and the perfect success that is impossible. That this is an important distinction is seen by a passing glance at the parade of the miscalled Triumphant in history. It is an all but endless line of victors, but triumph never adorns their banners. Attila the Hun rides into the rubble of Rome, King Henry of Sicily leads the Fourth Crusaders through the ensanguined mud of Jerusalem, Napoleon into Austerlitz and Egypt, Graziano struts through the battered streets of Addis Ababa, Mussolini leads his black-shirted fascists into Rome, Hitler into Paris, MacArthur into Tokyo, Eisenhower into Berlin. Victors all; but triumph still delays.

And if history has something to say to us, what do we learn from a probing into the inner secrets of the human spirit? The man on horseback thinks he has grown tall and swift. Victory is the heady wine men drink that intoxicates them with grandiose notions of triumph. It makes them unsteady; they topple easily when pushed off balance.

Once again, seeing victory in depth presents us with paradox.

For centuries we have heard this nonexaltation business, but we still will borrow a mount to ride among the crowds and hear about us, as long as it lasts, the reverberation of their applause. We talk now of the triumph of man over nature and point to the incredible new energies released by nuclear fission and fusion. This is victory; but is it triumph so long as it may be the precursor to man's planetary defeat?

We reserve, certainly in the experience of Jesus, the cross as the symbol of triumph. Here, ironically, the factor of victory seems to grow dim as the aspect of triumph fills the skies. Triumph within the gates of Jerusalem? No? Victory; yes, but triumph was to come on a bleak hill top, seven days later.

This means, of course, that death, on God's terms, provides us the ultimate of victory—which is the essence of triumph. And in order to understand *that* we must look at death—or disaster—within the dimension of depth.

15 THE CRISIS OF DEATH

Hark, glad songs of victory in the tents of the righteous: "The right hand of the Lord does valiantly, the right hand of the Lord is exalted, the right hand of the Lord does valiantly!" I shall not die, but I shall live, and recount the deeds of the Lord. The Lord has chastened me sorely, but he has not given me over to death. Open to me the gates of righteousness, that I may enter through them and give thanks to the Lord. PSALM 118:15-19

"Ev'body talk 'bout heav'n ain't goin' there." We have been trying to understand life's critical experiences in depth dimensions. How can we think of death as a crisis of life? Is it not rather its negation? However fuzzy the outlines of other opposites may be, even to careful scrutiny, the dichotomy of life and death has been whetted to cruel sharpness by the anguish, loss, bitterness and rebellion of countless mortals.

To think of death as a fathomless abyss that engulfs us if we cannot cross it is not to think of death in the dimensions of depth. To think of it as the antithesis and vanquishment of life or as an escape from mortality's incumbent pain; or to speak of it as beautifully as Thomas Wolfe put it:

To lose the earth you know, for greater knowing;
To lose the life you have, for greater life;
To leave the friends you loved, for greater loving;
To find a land more kind than home, more large than earth—

—Whereon the pillars of this earth are founded,
Toward which the conscience of the world is tending—
A wind is rising, and the rivers flow.[1]

is still to move only upon its surface, however graceful the motion.

Because it is difficult to confront this experience within its profound lengths and depths we tend to treat it with supercilious indifference as if it were unimportant; or we face it with anguished fear; or perhaps with frothy sentimentality; or we evade it and call it by euphemisms calculated to deceive us.

Life, we incline to say, is reasonable. Mysterious, to be sure; who, first seeing the primeval slime, could have predicted it? But not inherently absurd, despite its fascinating contradictions and ambiguities.

Is death, because it is neither mysterious nor unpredictable, less reasonable? Does it stand opposite the vital processes that are suspended when death touches the living organism? Is it the cancellation of life's victories or is death life's triumph?

What we know of the mind of Jesus as he faced death is considerable and yet inconclusive. One cannot know death in its finality until one has died and we still incline to regard skeptically the reports of those who have recrossed the spirit margin to speak of it. Except, of course, the reassurance we find in the resurrection of our Lord, the experience which sets life and death in such profound depths that no gaze has ever yet solved its ultimate mystery. What we do know, however, is that the resurrection witness was not merely the word of victory over death, it was the triumph of life.

[1] "A Stone, A Leaf, A Door," from *Poems by Thomas Wolfe,* selected and arranged by John S. Barnes, Scribner's, 1945. Used by permission of the publisher.

If, as we understand the Christian testimony, resurrection represents triumph and not merely victory, the door swings open on the reasonableness of life when seen in dimensions that are not only deep but in perspectives that are endless. Is it possible, looking at life with all our modern resources for understanding it, to affirm the reasonableness of endless life? In other words, is immortality reasonable?

(1)

Look first at the nature of the physical universe within which the most obvious aspects of life are set. There are two things we know about it: first that it is alive. We are not yet fully accustomed to think of this aliveness as infusing everything with vitality. So long habituated to the ideas of matter, energy, spirit as different components of the cosmic scheme, we not only have difficulty understanding them as the manifestation of one essence—radioactivity; we are moreover not a little repelled by the idea. Somehow it seems to rob mind and spirit of something unique and immutable to regard them as part of the chorus of dancing atoms that swirl tirelessly through something called space.

Not only is the essence of life indestructible radioactivity, its intention—as part of the universe—is expansive, endlessly growing to endlessly immeasurable magnitudes. How long it took to get as far as it has from the initial ember of celestial fire man's puny time calculations cannot tell us. How much farther and how long is—as we say, with proper reverence—in the mind of God.

Now any such understanding of the nature of life—its activity, indestructibility and elasticity all three understood in infinite relations to time and space—seems to turn us back into the hands of the mechanists from whom, of late, we thought we had escaped. But some of the mechanists will not have it so.

In the fall of 1954 there met in St. Louis a conference of scientists, philosophers, sociologists, publicists and politicians who undertook "to hammer out a general position on which the man of learning can stand." As the result of this astonishing meeting there were "redressed three misapprehensions to which science has tended to be a party."

First: Man is not only an object (thing). He is something that stands as a knower over against his own nature and the nature of the universe. His knowledge is not separate from, or irresponsible to, the thing known; neither is it determined by it. This, said the learned gentlemen, points materialism to the nearest exit. The understanding of man—his life, death and destiny—cannot be contained within the behavior of particles of radioactive energy.

Second: Man is not determined, in thought or act, by the orbital gyrations of energy constellations. He has powers that can interrupt the orbit of an electron, he can even blow an atom to bits and capture its exploding energies. This means he has ideas and an effective will to action. Thus along with materialism, determinism is shown the way to the door.

Third: Man has not a purely objective view of the world. He stands outside phenomena as a viewer but—concurrently—inside phenomena as something viewed. This softens the adversity between scientist and philosopher. The former asserts that the judgments of ethics, aesthetics, theology and philosophy are value judgments, subjective, relative and imprecise. In other words, no judgments at all—only opinions. The judgments of science, on the contrary, are empirical, objective, exact and therefore definitive. Thus the quarrel between the discursive and descriptive disciplines has continued. Scientism said value judgments are irrelevant, only judgments of fact—true or false—are dependable. When the conference consensus agreed that back behind all the empirical judgments of science there must first be made a value judgment that determines whether it is good or bad to seek to discover the true and false, logical positivism joined mechanism and materialism in moving toward the exit.

This is far from saying that one conference can alter the pattern of a century or more of thought. Nevertheless, it is clear that the three most formidable opponents of the acceptance of death as the triumph of life—or of the survival of the spirit beyond the vicissitudes of mortality—have been materialism, mechanism and positivism. If we cannot say they have been put to flight it can be said that rifts have been found in their armor long thought to be impervious.

(2)

Look now at the nature or structure of reason. Two basic assumptions underlie our efforts at disciplined thinking: first, that man has a capacity for sustained and logical thought. Limited certainly, and often far tighter than he admits; misdirected beyond doubt, and often more tragically than he suspects. But not to believe in man's capacity for thought or to protest its inferior importance is to use reason to prove reason's uselessness. This is the fallacy of antirationalism. [2]

The second assumption is that there is an explanation for everything. In this incredibly complex universe there are no inexplicable rags and tatters. No mystery floats through the cosmos; mystery lies only in man's limited understanding of some of the things he sees. This does not say that man can ever understand everything or the ultimate meaning of anything; only that to begin with the assumption that to the ultimate

---

[2] Augustine, in his *Soliloquies*, speaks of his "unbounded desire to apprehend truth not only by believing it but by understanding it."

mind there are pockets of cosmic irrationality is to stultify even human efforts at logical thinking.

There is reason for satisfaction in the limits set on reason. While man can and must learn, his reasoning function is hedged by the time-space continuum in which the mind can rove. He cannot get out of the space he occupies and see things non-spatially. Even memory and anticipation which transcend space and time operate only within space-time concepts. Our contentment with this comes from what appears to be a reasonable deduction; unless the function of reason, in the nature of things, is determined by space-time, opportunity for the full exercise of reason must be provided within non-space time. This suggests the exciting prospect that beyond what is known as physical (space time) life the living spirit will be able not only to pursue the answers that have eluded it but shall encounter questions for answering that the finite mind has never yet foreseen. Would that not be the triumph of wisdom over knowledge?

(3)

Consider once again the nature of personality. First of God: We cannot cure the anthropological limp of our minds as we walk toward Him nor can we disentangle Him from the space-time trellis up which we climb. Nevertheless, our first assumption about Him must be that He is timeless, eternal. Our second assumption is that He embodies in ultimate completeness the qualities which, as we discover them dimly in ourselves, we regard as the highest.

The inference that God is wisdom, power and love derives from our awareness that these are also man's creative qualities. To this degree our concept of God is a projection of ourselves outward toward the infinite. Therefore, it is impossible to believe that God would abandon the experiment of the universe unless there was a limit set on the divine power and wisdom necessary for its "completion."

We cannot find it congenial to accept the idea of the frustration of God; but we are well enough aware of our own. God does not die; we do. That is the drama both of man's defeat and of God's triumph. Can man's death also be triumphant? We refer again to the giant fact of man's reason in a reasonable cosmos. Equally important are the collateral facts of man's will and his emotion. Man's perverse will to live, his crazy satisfactions (feelings) with life even on the lowest levels, these are the perplexity alike of cynic and sage. Is this doomed, by the suspension of vital physical processes, to the melancholy annihilation that Bertrand Russell has predicted? Are we to say that man's capacity for love, faith and laughter are aberrant to the eternal order within which they provide him his highest temporal satisfactions? Or are these simply tag ends of melody, warmth, trust and ecstasy that drift endlessly through the senseless skies of forever?

Now nothing is clearer than that what we have been saying does not find its source in the historic episode of the resurrection. While we cannot be sure what ideas surged through the mind of the praying sufferer in the Garden of Olives, we cannot think that he was there composing his tormented soul with a rationale for immortality. When he suddenly stood up and said, "Rise, let us be going," he had not put Q.E.D. after a theorem solved by prayer, under the silent trees. Still less do we know what he knew and felt after the tomb had been vacated. Such intimations as are furnished us indicate little more than that while he was aware of persons and things within their familiar space-time context, he was also aware of a new dimension within which persons and things were different. How and why different we cannot know, not having died; but at least different—as we can see from the record—in his independence of them. This was more than victory over death, it was triumph over life.

While we confess to these necessary limitations on our understanding we must, nonetheless, point out that what has been said sets the disaster of death—as it is generally regarded—within dimensions of depth that at least give it dignity. Put within the boundless immensities of a throbbing, expanding physical universe in which energy is inexhaustible and in the nature of which man participates, dying is rescued from the superficiality of simply going somewhere—to eternal bliss or perdition. It becomes transformation—triumph, indeed. Similarly death seen as a human experience which releases the spirit from the finite questions and answers of space time and ushers it into the limitless ranges to which the nature of reason must lay claim, this we insist is not a blackout into emptiness; it is the ultimate illumination. Not the victory of human intelligence but the triumph of reason.

And lastly, the effort to comprehend the nature of God by way of our awareness of ourselves—insufficient as this is certain to prove—sets both God and man within a dimension that indicates an ultimate identification of the two, in understanding (faith), feeling (love), trust (will) which is made possible only as man walks through the portal that leaves behind all the separation—whether great or slight—that he has felt between God and himself and his fellows. Is not this more than man's victory over his humanity? It is his triumph over his finitude.

In one of the best-kept secrets of the physical world we have something that suggests itself as a parable of what we have been saying: photosynthesis. It is "the process by which the energy of the sun is captured and converted to the uses of the living cell. It is . . . the beginning process in the transfer of atoms from the inorganic world to the organic. It serves as the very bridge of life—the bridge by which star stuff passes over and becomes life stuff." [3] This is the language of science discreetly using metaphor. May it not be loaned to us as a metaphor for suggesting something about an even better-kept secret —death? Why shall we not speak of death as the process by which the energy of the mortal cell is captured and converted into the uses of the energies of God? Death, thus conceived, is the very bridge of life—the bridge by which man-dust passes over and becomes God-stuff! While there is death there is hope. [4]

> "The Lord has chastened me sorely, but he has not given me over to death. Open to me the gates of righteousness, that I may enter through them and give thanks to the Lord" (Ps. 118:19).

[3] George W. Gray, "Our Bridge from the Sun," in *Harper's Magazine,* Sept., 1955, p. 64.

[4] This has doubtless been said many times by as many people. Aldous Huxley is the latest user in his novel, *The Genius and the Godess,* Harper, 1955.

In 1954, in the San Fruttuoso Bay near Portofino, Italy, an eight-foot statue of Christ was lowered to a concerete foundation fifty-six feet beneath the surface of the bay. It was piously designated, said *Life* (September 13, 1954), "as the 'Christ of the Depth,' to be seen by fishermen and pleasure boat sailors as they pass between their home ports and fishing grounds."

Within the past twelve months the statue, arms uplifted in the conventional attitude of prayer, has become blurred, "under the laerys of algae and mollusks, and even a couple of sea urchins." It was necessary, if the statue was not to lose its outlines in the soft shadows of the deep, for "four stout swimmers to [undertake what] promises to be an annual chore. Equipped with masks, foot flippers and stiff brushes they dived below the surface to comb the barnacles out and give the statue a brisk scrubbing up." Predicted *Life:* "It will take until the end of the month to finish the job."

It is conceivable, of course, that Jesus, the experience of discipleship and the critical experiences of life can be sunk so far beneath the surface that they are altogether lost to sight, or seen with outlines blurred by incrustation—layers of heedlessness, or sentimentality, or superstition. Thus, those who "pass between their home ports and fishing grounds" will not much longer look down when they pass, and soon forget altogether.

The statue in San Fruttuoso Bay will take a month's scrubbing before its outlines are clean and clear again. And this will be "an annual chore." How long and how often will be the chore of those who, having seen deeply, seek to keep visible for others the outlines that mark the true meanings of Lordship, discipleship and human destiny?

Date Due